THE BACK HOME SERIES

"In *We Come from Good Stock*, Kay Oring transports us back in time to a vanished world, as she engagingly retraces the history, branch by branch, of her ancestors. At its heart, these stories are about people dreaming of, searching for, and creating new homes in a new land. This moving book inspires us to explore the stories found in our own family trees, wherever we are from."

—Joelle Frazer
author of *The Territory of Men*

"Kay Oring has written an engaging account of the long-lived Levi Oakes and his descendants (Kay is one of them). According to one biographer, the Oakes achieved status in their communities and lived decently, but never strived to stand out. The stories of their celebrations of good fortune and bearing tragedies with grace give color and life to the history of settlement, logging, and farming in the early days of Wisconsin's statehood."

—Margaret Liddiard
author of *Tilting to Listen*

We Come from Good Stock

a family history

KAY OAKES ORING

CORNERSTONE PRESS
UNIVERSITY OF WISCONSIN-STEVENS POINT

Cornerstone Press, Stevens Point, Wisconsin 54481
Copyright © 2024 Kay Oakes Oring
www.uwsp.edu/cornerstone

Printed in the United States of America by
Point Print and Design Studio, Stevens Point, Wisconsin

Library of Congress Control Number: 2024935798
ISBN: 978-1-960329-40-0

Cover photo: Sons of Levi and Mary Potter Oakes, 1923. L to R, Top row:
William, Charles, Fred M., Silas. L to R, Bottom row: Hannah, wife of Fred M.;
Annie, wife of Charles; Tena, second wife of Silas.

This is a work of nonfiction. All of the events in this book are true to the best of
the author's memory. Some names and identifying features have been changed to
protect the identity of certain parties. The author in no way represents any company,
corporation, or brand, mentioned herein. The views expressed in this memoir are
solely those of the author.

Cornerstone Press titles are produced in courses and internships offered by the
Department of English at the University of Wisconsin–Stevens Point.

DIRECTOR & PUBLISHER
Dr. Ross K. Tangedal

EXECUTIVE EDITORS
Jeff Snowbarger, Freesia McKee

EDITORIAL DIRECTOR
Ellie Atkinson

SENIOR EDITORS
Brett Hill, Grace Dahl

PRESS STAFF
Madalyn Carpenter, Chloe Cieszynski, Alex Diaz, Kirsten Faulkner, Kenzie
Kierstyn, Sophie McPherson, Kylie Newton, Eva Nielson, Josh Paulson, Natalie
Reiter, Lauren Rudesill, Katie Schimke, Anthony Thiel, Chloe Verhelst, Ava
Willett, Cam Williams

In Memory of Levi Shane Oakes

July 27, 1959 – September 19, 2016

Great, great grandson of Levi Jefferson Oakes

To all eleven generations of Oakes's in the United States

CONTENTS

LIST OF FIGURES

PREFACE

I was born in 1940 and spent my first eight years in the embrace of grandparents, aunts, uncles, and cousins on farms in west central Wisconsin. There was no daycare, no preschool, no kindergarten. And no TV. I absorbed many adult conversations and family stories. These stories have intrigued me for as long as I remember. From the stories I created conversations to bring the history to life. Aided by letters, photos from family, and internet research on Wisconsin history that helped set the events of the times.

Fred Arthur Oakes continued the Oakes family history that was started by his eldest sister, Esther Oakes Carson. Starting in the 1930s, Uncle Fred talked to the children and grandchildren of his grandfather, Levi Jefferson Oakes, and Great Uncle Timothy Oakes, with the goal of recording all the descendants. When he retired in 1961, and had more time to continue, he realized no descendants had ever gone back to Massachusetts or Maine where the family began its North American odyssey. He set off in his Ford sedan and small travel trailer for Maine to track down records and descendants of Nathaniel Oak who came to Massachusetts about 1660 (the name changed from Oak to Oaks to Oakes). He traveled from Idaho (where he was living at the time) to Maine to California visiting relatives and examining documents. What a task he set for himself. With no copy machines, he painstakingly hand-copied court documents and church records. He published his findings in a book: *Oakes and Relatives 1974*.

In 1943, Esther Oakes Carson (my aunt, and Fred Arthur's sister), wrote to Dr. Mary Lowell, a genealogist in Boston, Massachusetts, asking her to research the Oak, Oaks, Oakes family in New England. They carried on a lively correspondence for several years. In one letter to Esther, Dr. Lowell wrote, "You have some excellent strains of blood in the Oakes and Crocketts, and I congratulate you." That sentiment was expressed by family members, too.

Fred Arthur and his siblings laughed that their Grandpa Levi said, "We come from good stock." That opinion was expressed by Henry Lebbeus Oak, in his 1906 book, *Oak, Oaks, Oakes: Family Register, Nathaniel Oak and Three Generations of His Descendants in Both Male and Female Lines*. He wrote:

> "...all generations have been for the most part farmers, mechanics, and small traders in humble circumstances and unknown beyond the limits of the communities where they have lived. The family has been generally respectable, the vicious and worthless being almost as rare as the prominent and learned and rich. A respectable percentage have been entrusted with public functions in town and church. The average of respectability has been high. Industry and integrity have been prevailing characteristics. Quiet reserve and modest pretentions have been the rule. Local prominence has been earned not assumed, and there has been a general tendency on the part of most to 'mind their own business.'

In politics, religion, and other non-essentials the Oaks have differed according to environment; they have never been extreme partisans or fanatics."

The Oakes I knew were mostly farmers and understood that having good stock was important to success. Being healthy and honest, upstanding citizens was important. The farm metaphors crept into everyday conversations and tickled or annoyed me. My grandfather, in mentioning a bitchy young woman, would call her "that young heifer." Uncle Leonard would tease me that my eyes were like "two sheep turds in a bowl of milk." That would start a discussion that my dark complexion and black eyes must be inherited from my great-great-great-grandmother, Lydia Brown Oaks (1765-1849), whose black hair and eyes were remarkable enough to be passed down in family stories. Her family came from southern France. "You know those people are dark complexioned," Uncle Fred said. This in contrast to the fair, blue-eyed Oakes from England or Wales.

Much of Uncle Fred's book is lists of begots with stories tucked in from people he knew personally or heard from relatives he met on his travels. I was especially intrigued by stories of my great-grandparents, Levi Jefferson Oakes and Mary Potter Heacock, with lists of birth dates and marriages. It struck me that Mary Potter was only 14 years old when she married her first husband, John Heacock. He sent her (at age 16 and pregnant) ahead of him from northern Pennsylvania to Milwaukee, Wisconsin, saying he would follow to make a new life in Wisconsin, but he abandoned her. What an amazing start for my family story!

1.

Alone, 1850

"In three words, I can sum up everything I've learned about life: It goes on."

—Robert Frost

The ship's horn blasted as gangplanks were lowered onto the Milwaukee dock. It was a warm September day in 1850. Passengers streamed down and rushed to claim baggage. At the street entrance, people waited for arrivals, many of whom were immigrants looking for opportunities in the new state. Wisconsin became a state in 1848. Some came from Maine, New York, and Massachusetts; many came from Norway, Sweden, and Germany. A cacophony of shouted languages assaulted one's ears.

Ox-drawn wagons and horse-drawn drays lined the street above the dock, waiting for runners who were sent to the dock to secure passengers. As soon as the runners waved that they had passengers, the wagon or dray drivers headed down to take immigrants up Huron Street where there were hotels and boarding houses. The Norwegian immigrants were harder to move as their trunks had rounded lids that could not be stacked. These trunks were painted with intricate rosemaling designs. Immigrants usually stayed a few days while they sorted out what to do, where to go, and how to get there. Milwaukee was a bustling port of entry of 20,000 new residents. Immigrants could purchase supplies—flour, sugar, lard, coffee, and tea. At the hardware shop they could buy axes, saws, draw knives, peavies, and other tools to prepare logs for building. If they had sufficient cash, they could purchase a team of oxen and a wagon.

Among the crowd was a petite young woman barely 5 feet tall. Her delicate features and ivory skin contrasted her thick, dark brown hair, parted in the middle, and pulled back into a curled-under bun. Her dress was navy blue cotton featuring "Leg o' Mutton" sleeves; the bodice gathered at the waist with a long, full skirt; at the neckline was a white lace collar. The outfit was set off by dressy, black lace, fingerless gloves, as were the fashion of the day. She dressed carefully, knowing her husband liked her to dress with style.

Tiny Mary Potter Heacock was often mistaken for a child. The anxious waiting crowd pushed and shoved her aside. The odor of horse and oxen dung wafting up from the muddy street left her feeling nauseated and dizzy. She leaned against a lamppost, standing on her tiptoes, craning to see. "Surely he will come today," she thought. Her large, brown eyes searched the rush of passengers for John. A tall man in a stylish silk top hat and black frock coat charged through the crowd. Mary's heart skipped a beat, "John?" His back was turned toward her, so she wasn't sure. He stopped and spoke to a woman wearing a smart maroon traveling suit and matching maroon hat with an ostrich plume. The woman carried an infant wrapped in a gray wool blanket. He turned to reveal his face—no, not John.

She turned her attention to scanning for silk top hats, as John would be dressed as a gentleman. She waited until there were no more passengers and the crowd dissipated. Dejected, she slowly approached the entrance where the purser stood marking his ledger. "Excuse me, sir."

The purser glanced up, "Yes?"

"Was John Heacock on this ship?"

Thumbing through his volume and without looking up, he curtly replied, "Nope."

Mary stood still, not sure what to do. Waves of nausea came over her and tears slowly rolled down her cheeks.

The purser looked up and this time really looked at her, his tone softer, "Is it your father you're looking for?"

Mary shook her head and whispered, "No, my husband." She fled down the boardwalk. She stopped to catch her breath. Her thoughts rushed, "Where is he? Why did he do this? What am I to do?" She slowly walked on, reviewing the events of the past few weeks:

John had burst through the back door, waving a pamphlet in her face. "Wisconsin is the future! Just listen to this: 'Men will want to bring their brides or wives and wee ones to participate in the joyful life of a home in the prairie wilds of Pierce County—their hearts as light and buoyant as the eagles' flight.'"

Mary grabbed the pamphlet, "Where did you get this?"

John removed his top hat and overcoat, walked to the front door, and hung them carefully on the wooden rack. He returned to the kitchen, "Remember, I told you last week about the men traveling throughout the Northeast, extolling the opportunities of Wisconsin, especially that of Pierce County and the Prescott area?"

Mary nodded.

"I went to hear them out. They have lots of land for sale around Prescott. Soon the land will be sold, and opportunities gone. I signed a contract to buy one of their parcels."

"What?!" Mary exclaimed, her hands flying to her cheeks, her eyes bulging and her face flushing. She stood in shocked silence while John continued.

"Don't worry. We may choose which parcel when we get there. I have it all arranged. Next Wednesday you'll go ahead on the boat from Buffalo through the Great Lakes to Milwaukee. I will close up here and follow you."

"By the horn spoon, what am I supposed to do until you get there?" Mary sobbed.

"There are good boarding houses near the dock where you can stay."

There was no arguing with John. As she packed, he brought gold coins. He instructed, "Mary, it will be safer for you to carry this money. Sew pockets on the inside of your petticoat to hide it."

Mary cried as she sewed, sorted, and packed. On Wednesday the boat sailed, carrying her off to the unknown.

* * *

Now, after two weeks, he had not arrived. Slowly walking on, she pondered what to do.

As she approached the boarding house, the proprietress, Mrs. Norris, was on the side porch shaking rugs. She frowned as she watched Mary approach. Under her breath, she muttered, "There's a wee one in the oven for sure. That no good husband didn't arrive again. How could he do that to her?"

As Mary walked up the front porch steps, Mrs. Norris called, "Mary, I have the kettle on. How about a cup of tea?"

Mary's eyes were troubled, and her brow furrowed. She gave a wan smile and nodded, opened the front door, went to the parlor, and sat down with a sigh.

Mrs. Norris pushed open the door from the kitchen to the parlor. She carried a tray with a teapot, two china cups and saucers, two teaspoons, a plate of scones, a pitcher of milk, and a sugar bowl. She placed the tray on the table, smiling at Mary. "I think this is just what you need." She poured the tea and offered milk and sugar.

"Thank you. I'll have both."

They sipped their tea.

"So, your husband didn't arrive today?"

Mary only shook her head. In her lap, her fingers were laced and pressed together so tightly the knuckles were white. Her shoulders sagged.

They sat in silence for a few minutes. Mrs. Norris tried again, "When is the wee one due?"

Mary startled, almost spilling her tea. Her eyes opened wide, "You know?"

Mrs. Norris smiled sympathetically, set down her teacup and patted Mary's hand, "Oh, I can tell. Women stand and walk differently. And you're not feeling well. The morning sickness does go away, my dear."

Mary burst into tears. She sobbed while Mrs. Norris patted her hand. Mary tried to stop crying. Reaching into her sleeve and pulling out a fresh white linen handkerchief, she dabbed her eyes and blew her nose. "I don't know what's wrong. John has been so cold since I told him I'm with child. I've tried to be a good wife, but it's hard to please him. He was adamant that I come first and wait for him. I can't just wait here."

"Have you been married long?" Mrs. Norris inquired.

"It was two years ago; what a day that was. I was fourteen years old and so scared." The tears rolled down her cheeks.

Mrs. Norris bit her tongue, inhaled deeply, and softly asked, "Where is your family, my dear?"

"My parents are in Pennsylvania, but my sister, Mildred, lives in Prescott. Is it far from here?"

"I don't know that town. Do you know what's nearby?"

"Mildred wrote that it is where the St. Croix River flows into the Mississippi."

"Land sakes! That is very far. It's all the way over by Minnesota Territory."

Mary was thoughtful. Finishing her tea and setting the cup and saucer back on the table, she resolved, "I reckon I should go to my sister in Prescott." Then her voice wavered, "But how?"

"Mr. Smythe, over at the livery, should be able to help. The stagecoach stops there."

"I'll go tomorrow. Thank you for the tea." Mary rose and wearily climbed the stairs to her room. How much will it cost? Fortunately, she had money. She slipped out of her petticoat and laid it on the bed. She took the coins from the pockets she had carefully sewn. She had $20. That should be plenty to get to Prescott. She returned the larger coins to the pockets, keeping ten coppers, two bits, and a gold dollar to put in her purse. She sighed, "I'm plum tuckered out." She slipped into her nightgown and slid under the covers. Pulling the cool, white linen sheets up to her nose and breathing the fresh, clean scent, she slept.

Mary awakened right pert. Jumping out of bed, she splashed cold water from the basin on her face and dried it. Quickly dressing, she brushed her hair and deftly rolled a bun, securing it at the nape of her neck with long hairpins, grabbed her coat and fairly flew down the stairs. She was thrilled to be taking action no matter how hard. She headed out back to the necessary (outhouse) and returned just as the breakfast bell rang. She entered the dining room and hung her coat on a hook by the door. Other guests were arriving. Everyone smiled and said "Mornin'" and nodded. Mary took a place at the table just as Mrs. Norris arrived with a huge plate of golden, steaming flapjacks.

"Well, well, don't you look perky this morning?" Mrs. Norris grinned at her.

Mary finished her breakfast and walked to the livery, invigorated by the crisp autumn air and sparkling sunshine. The double doors were open. Inside, the place was a hub of activity as horses, mules, and oxen were harnessed. A short man with a bushy gray beard noticed her and tipped his cap, "Mornin' miss."

"I'm looking for Mr. Smythe."

"That's me."

"Mrs. Norris over at the boarding house said you could probably help me."

"Oh, she did, did she?" he chuckled. "Well, what do you need?"

"I need to go to Prescott. Mrs. Norris said you'd know the best way."

"Hmmm. You take the stagecoach to Madison. There you get an ox wagon to the Wisconsin River at Sauk City. There you can catch a keelboat down to Bridgeport. That's on the Mississippi. From there, the steamers run right up to Prescott."

"When does the stage leave for Madison?"

"There's one tomorrow morning at seven."

"I have a trunk. Can someone fetch it at the boarding house?"

"Sure thing. Be ready at 6:30."

"Thank you, Mr. Smythe." Mary extended her hand. Mr. Smythe quickly wiped his hand on his pants and took her dainty hand in his large rough one, shaking it gently. Mary skipped back to the boarding house smiling, noticing the red maples rustling in the breeze. "Mildred is goin'a be so surprised," Mary giggled right out loud.

Fig. 1 Mary's approximate route

2.

From Milwaukee to Prescott, Wisconsin

"The way of the pioneer is always rough."
—Harvey S. Firestone

Promptly at 6:30 the next morning, two young teamsters arrived on a horse-drawn wagon. Mary was ready and waiting on the front porch. The men loaded her trunk into the wagon.

Mrs. Norris opened the door and smiled, "Best of luck to you. Take care of yourself." She handed a small paper package tied with string to Mary. "I fixed some biscuits and cheese for you." She raised her arms and enfolded Mary in a bear hug.

Mary clung to the older woman, "Thank you for all your kindness, Mrs. Norris. I'll write to you when I get to Prescott." She walked to the waiting wagon, where one of the men boosted her up to the seat. She turned and waved as the wagon rolled down the street.

The stagecoach was loading when Mary arrived at the livery. The men transferred her trunk to the roof of the coach. She paid them four coppers. The stagecoach driver was a tall, burly man with a broad brimmed hat. "Where to, Miss?"

"Madison, please," Mary answered.

"That will be $1."

"How long will it take?"

"Usually two days, if it doesn't rain."

The stagecoach, a Vermont Sanderson, had a rounded bottom and hung from long steel springs, so the coach rocked back and forth. Passengers wedged in and the mailbag was handed to the driver as he climbed to the seat on top. At first the road was flat and smooth. In low muddy spots or across bogs, the road was corduroyed (layers of small trees were laid across the area and dirt piled over them). A fast team of four horses or mules walked about 4 miles per hour. Hence, after about two and a half hours (10 miles), it was time to change teams. As the horses halted, two hostlers ran out to loosen the traces. The released animals headed for the long, low shed barns while the fresh team took their places. The traces were tightened, the boys stood back, and the stagecoach lurched forward. The whole operation took about five minutes.

Tavern houses or stagecoach inns sprung up along the routes at about 10-mile intervals to cater to the needs of drivers, animals, and passengers. Mary was thankful to get out of the stagecoach at the first stop, a two-story New England style tavern. She stood for a moment to admire the lean-to wings and long veranda along the front facing the road. Chairs lined the veranda where people waited for the stage. It was also a place to exchange gossip of the road and new developments in land, timber, and trade. Here one could rub shoulders with immigrants, state-of-Mainers, speculators, farmers, surveyors, government officials, timber cruisers, teamsters, and lumberjacks. Too soon, the driver called, "Stage leaving." A fresh team of mules set out rapidly. Between the stage stops were mail stations. With a clatter of hoofs, the coach drew alongside the station. The driver threw down the mail sack and the stationmaster tossed up the outgoing mail. This routine repeated until six when the stagecoach stopped for the night.

Mary was weary and chilled when the stage finally stopped for the night. "May I warm myself in the kitchen?" she asked the proprietor.

He nodded. Mary stepped into the cozy kitchen and held her hands over the cook stove. Just then the hausfrau returned from the dining room carrying a hand full of dirty knives and forks. She removed the cover on the tea kettle and plunged the utensils into the boiling water, swished them, hastily dried them on a dirty cloth and dropped them into a crock on the shelf. As Mary watched, the woman picked up the tea kettle and poured the water into the coffee pot. Horrified, Mary vowed to refrain from coffee, but she was so chilled she drank it anyway. A hot meal and a bed in the women's room were welcome.

The next morning, Mary was startled from her sound sleep by the breakfast bell. She hurriedly dressed and went downstairs. At 7 a.m. the driver announced, "Stage leaving!"

Mary was suddenly overcome by nausea.

The driver grabbed her shoulder, "Wait a minute. I can't take sick people."

Mary stared at him in disbelief, "What?"

"You got a fever?"

"No, I'm just a little queasy."

"Well, I can't take a chance. The inspector will fine me for taking folks with cholera or typhoid. You better stay here."

"I don't have those," Mary protested.

Before she could go on, a lady stepped forward. "There's nothing wrong with her—she's just with child. She'll be fine soon."

The driver looked at Mary skeptically, "Well now, what do you know!" He turned to the lady, "You'd better be right. I can't afford any fines."

What a beautiful September day it was. The sun rose and melted the heavy frost. They rode through thick forests of sugar maple, their crimson leaves trembling in the breeze. Inside the stage, flies swarmed around a sick child with diarrhea. Mary covered her nose with her handkerchief against the stench.

The stage arrived in Madison that night. Mary inquired of the tavern proprietor, "How do I go to Sauk City?"

He scratched his head, "There are freighters leaving from the livery down the street every morning. You probably can catch a ride. Be there at 6:30."

Too tired to eat, Mary went straight to bed.

At the livery the next morning, Mary watched with interest. The freighter was a long wagon pulled by four oxen. It was loaded with the belongings of a family moving west from Illinois.

The driver said there was room for her trunk. He chuckled, "You can sit on top or walk—whatever pleases you." The crisp morning air was invigorating, so Mary walked until she was weary, then climbed up to ride by the driver, who chattered away. In a few places there were small fresh mounds of dirt to which the driver pointed. "Graves," he announced, "probably swamp fever." Mary was overcome with sadness. She closed her eyes and pictured the suffering of the little ones, the absence of doctors, death, burial, and grief of leaving those fresh, heaped mounds. The 30 miles to Sauk City took two days.

At the dock on the Wisconsin River, freighters were being loaded with supplies from the keelboats; other freighters were being unloaded onto keelboats.

Mary's trunk was loaded, and she stepped aboard, grinning. "Just a couple more days and I'll see Mildred," she thought.

The crew was laughing, joking, and whistling. Mary watched with amusement. One, a boy about her age with red hair and freckles, noticed her and came over, "Greetings," he tipped his hat. "Name's Jerimiah. Want to know how this gal works?" He continued, "These keelboats are about 60 feet long, 10 feet wide, and 4 feet deep. Come, I'll show you."

As they walked, he pointed to the canvas top over wooden frames that covered about three-quarters of the boat. "This keeps supplies and people dry."

They moved over to one side with a running board 2 feet wide. Lying along the railing were 16-foot poles with steel points on one end and knobs on the other.

Jerimiah continued, "These poles propel the boat. Starting at the bow, we set the point on the river bottom, lean into the knob with our shoulders and walk to the stern. Then we pick up our poles and run back to the bow. Goin' down river today will be a snap. The current jus' floats us along. Comin' back tomorrow'll be work. We'll need 16 chaps and the pilot. Eight of us pole at a time—four on each side."

Before they could continue, someone called, "Hey, Jerimiah, get over here." Jerimiah tipped his hat and ran off to attend to his duties.

That night they reached the Mississippi River where the steamboat, Nominee, was already docked, ready for loading on its northward trip. Mary said goodbye to travelers who were heading elsewhere. The passengers going to northern Wisconsin or Minnesota Territory boarded the Steamship. Mary paid two bits for a seat on the side deck. She was pleased that she had the extra money for the seat, so she didn't have to descend to steerage with the cows and pigs.

Mary, along with many passengers, stood on the front deck all morning. The steamboat's horn blasted as the ship eased into the moorings at the Prescott dock. Most of the passengers were New Englanders starting new lives on the frontier. Excitement was high. Mary noticed the chalk cliffs above the muddy Mississippi. From the right, the clear waters of the St. Croix River rushed into the Mississippi and soon turned brown. On the delta between the rivers were huge piles of logs and lumber and a few buildings. Above the cliffs were a couple of houses. Prescott at last! People on land scurried toward the steamer. "It shouldn't be too hard to find Mildred," she smiled to herself, "Won't she be surprised?"

Unloading the boat took several hours. Mary watched for her trunk. It seemed so small compared to the household belongings of other passengers. Finally, she spotted it and ran to claim it. Men and boys were waiting with wagons to assist the new arrivals.

"May I help you, miss?" A boy about twelve stepped toward her.

"Yes, that's my trunk." She pointed to it.

"That's all you have?"

"And this carpet bag."

"Where are you going?"

"I'm looking for Mildred Travis. She has a boarding house here."

"Oh! She lives just over there," the boy pointed up the street toward the cliffs. He eyed the small trunk. "No use wasting an ox wagon for that." He took a handcart out of the wagon. "Do you mind walking?"

"Oh, no," Mary replied.

The boy loaded the trunk and carpet bag onto the cart, and they started off. The road was muddy from a recent rain. Mary picked up her skirt to keep it out of the mud. Her heart pounded in anticipation. It had been so long since she had seen her sister. They arrived at the house. The boy set her trunk on the porch. "Thank you," she smiled, and paid him two pennies.

The boy nodded, "Thanks. Good luck to you." He turned and hurried back down the street.

Mary knocked on the door. Mildred opened it and stood in shocked silence. Mary's eyes danced, "Well, aren't you going to say 'welcome?!'"

"Mary, is it really you?"

"Yes, of course it's me."

The sisters fell into each other's arms hugging and crying. They stepped apart to wipe their tears. Mildred had a million questions, "How did you get here? Why are you alone? Where's John?" Mildred fired questions faster than Mary could answer. "Come in, come in, dear sister. I need to be fixin' supper for the boarders, so come sit at the table and tell me everything."

"Oh, I'll help," Mary responded. "I just need to change out of my traveling clothes."

The sisters talked, laughed, and cried as they worked. "Were you sick on the way, Mary?" Mildred asked.

"If you call morning sickness sick, then yes," Mary laughed.

"Land sakes do tell! When is the baby due?"

"I think in March."

"I'm so happy that you weren't sick. Were there lots of sick passengers on the boat?"

"A few. I stayed on the deck for the fresh air."

Mildred nodded in approval, "That's good. The last boat coming from St. Louis really had the sickness. They had to go ashore near Dubuque to bury the dead from the cholera. No one wanted the survivors here, but our fresh air will cure most anything."

"Oh, there was lots of cholera in Milwaukee. Before we could get on the boat in Buffalo and then before we could get off the boat in Milwaukee, we had to be checked by a doctor. He said that last year a boat brought a whole load of immigrants with cholera. Now captains are fined for bringing sick passengers. The stagecoach driver didn't want me on board. He said I looked a little peaked and he couldn't afford a fine. He seemed dubious about me until a lady vouched for me."

"Thank the Lord for that," Mildred replied.

They turned their attention to serving supper. The dining room was filled by joking lumbermen. They ate the pot roast, browned potatoes, onions, and rutabagas with gusto and devoured the apple pie.

After the dishes were washed and put away, Mildred made tea. They sat down at the kitchen table and Mildred demanded, "Now tell me about what happened."

"It was in late August when John announced we were coming here. He said he had signed a contract for some land. He insisted that I leave first and wait for him in Milwaukee."

"What a scoundrel! That takes the cake--sendin' you off alone," Mildred snorted.

"After two weeks, I didn't know what to do except find you. I left word at the boarding house in Milwaukee for John. Maybe something happened and he'll come."

"Land sakes, I don't know about that."

"Now it's your turn, Mildred. What has your life been like? Where is Tom?"

"When we got here two years ago, there was nothing. Tom quickly was hired on bringing logs down river. With the long winters, he thought if we had a boarding house it would help. He worked in exchange for the lumber at the mill and built this house last year. It is a blessing for me since the accident."

"Sakes alive, what accident?" Mary sat up straight to listen.

"You know Tom was nimble and quick, so he often worked to free up log jams. It was early last spring, just as the ice was breaking up. The St. Croix was full of huge chunks. There was a big jam of logs and ice. They had worked on it all morning. Tom was pushing against a log with his peavey when the whole kit and caboodle broke loose. They said he danced on a rolling log mighty pretty, but then it struck a chuck of ice and threw him into the froth. He froze to death before he could get out."

"Oh, Mildred, I'm so sorry," Mary rose and crossed the kitchen to hug her sister.

3.

Settling In: Fall/Winter 1850-51

"The hard soil and four months of snow make the inhabitants of the northern temperate zone wiser and abler that his fellow who enjoys the fixed smile of the tropics."

—Ralph Waldo Emerson

Winter arrived suddenly with a Blue Northern in early November. The blizzard raged for two days. Ice formed on the edges of the rivers. A steamboat arrived from St. Louis bringing the last load of settlers until spring, plus winter supplies: flour, sugar, salt, cornmeal, and bolts of muslin. The lumberjacks headed north for the winter to log along the St. Croix River; they'd be back with a whoop and a holler with the spring log drive. A neighbor brought a load of firewood. Mary and Mildred scurried to stack it in the woodshed.

With only an occasional guest, they closed off the upstairs to save heat. A peddler stopped by. "I'm a wonderin' if you'd take these fine wool fleeces for a hot meal and bed for the night?"

Mildred examined the fleeces and agreed. "This will make a cozy baby quilt and we can spin the other for mittens, scarves, and caps."

At the mention of a baby, Mary caught her breath. Yes, there was a baby growing inside—she felt it move yesterday. Overcome with waves of fear and doubt, she just bowed her head.

"What is it?" Mildred asked sharply.

"The baby moved."

"Land sakes. That's a joy to be sure. We'd better get started making that quilt."

On cold days, they pulled out the rag bag, found scraps of gingham, cut squares to sew for the quilt. As they worked, Mary argued with herself, "Maybe I should write to John, so he'll know where I am. No, he'll know where I am." In the end she took the quill pen, ink bottle and paper from the shelf, and wrote:

Dear John,

After waiting for two weeks in Milwaukee, I made my way to Prescott. I am living with Mildred and helping at the boarding house. I will wait here for you.
Hoping this finds you in good health,

Your wife, Mary

She sealed the envelope and walked to the postmaster's house, which served as the post office.

"Good mornin' miss," he greeted her.

"Good mornin' to you. I need a penny stamp, please. Do you think the post carrier will get here soon?"

"Now that the roads are frozen, they'll have no problem as they can use cutters and know they'll get through. The worst times are spring and fall when muddy roads are impassable."

* * *

By Christmas, Prescott hunkered down with a handful of families. Both the Mississippi and St. Croix rivers were frozen to depths of 3 feet or more, creating smooth highways. Men drilled holes for ice fishing and the children shoveled snow off areas for skating. A couple of men dug a cave into the north bank for storing ice. They sawed chunks of river ice as big as tree trunks, piled them on a sled, took them to the cave and covered them with straw, where the ice blocks stayed until summer when they were cut up and sold. On clear cold nights, the ice talked.

"Hear that?" Mildred inquired.

"Yes, what is it?"

"It's the ice. When the temperatures drop below zero, ice contracts, cracks, and booms. Come on, let's go outside."

Bundled against the frigid night, they listened. The eerie sound sent shivers down Mary's spine as it echoed across the river. Looking skyward, Mildred pointed out the northern lights. The colors—green, red, yellow, purple— streaked up the sky, ever changing. Mary stood in awe and pondered her plight. She still didn't know what happened to John. Her bulging abdomen reminded her that soon there would be a baby to consider. Then what? She sighed and pulled her scarf around her face.

In January, the postmaster brought a fat envelope for Mary from a Mr. John Stone, Esq., Buffalo, N.Y. "How strange," Mary thought. She opened it and read, "In the case of John Heacock vs. Mary Potter Heacock." She scanned the pages. Her heart skipped a beat: divorce, final were the words that jumped off the pages. At the end it was dated September 10, 1850. Mary flushed with anger and hollered, "Dash it all, that was just a day after I left

Buffalo. That no good buffoon! Why he never intended to come!" She pursed her lips and stared at the page. "How could he do this?"

Mildred grabbed the pages from her and read what she could. Most of it seemed gibberish. "By the horn spoon, that yellow-bellied snake! You should row him up Salt's River," she exclaimed.

Mary shook herself and tears rolled down her cheeks, "I never fit in with the Heacock's high falutin' ways." She stood, curtsied, and pranced around, lifting her nose in the air. "John and his family imagined themselves aristocrats. I never dressed to please them. I didn't talk the way they wanted. The books John's father gave me weren't anything I could read," she grimaced. "You know, his father, a Methodist minister, expected us to be in church every Sunday, dressed just so. His mother always bought a new hat for me each season so I would be fashionable, but I was just a mudsill in her mind."

Mildred was indignant, "Pshaw! He ought to be taking care of you and the baby. He isn't worth a fart in a whirlwind."

Mary wiped her tears, "I can see the elephant." She folded the document and replaced it in the envelope. In the future, Mary would look back and say, "It was just as well John left."

As they finished up the dishes, Mildred laughed. "Your description of John's family reminds me of the city cousin and country cousin jokes people are telling, not in polite company. You see, the country cousin went to visit his city cousin and they were invited out to a dinner. The country cousin didn't want to go because he wouldn't know how to dress, act or how to eat properly. 'I'll loan you a dinner frock. Just follow what I do,' the city cousin said. The country cousin watched his city cousin carefully and followed all he did and said. All went well until the hostess passed the platter of meat and potatoes a second time. The city cousin said, 'No thank you, my efficiency is already fanciful.' The country cousin stared at him not believing what he had heard, shook his head and said, 'No thank you, I've already shit my pants full.'"

The sisters collapsed in laughter 'til they cried. "That's the Heacocks!" Mary giggled, then grew somber. "So, I'm a divorced woman." She gave a hollow laugh, "What God has joined together, let no man put asunder. Humph. And John called himself a man of God." Her tone turned bitter, "Now there's a child to raise with no father."

"By golly, we're not goin' to hang up the fiddle. We'll manage," Mildred patted her hand.

Spring 1851

On March 13, 1851, Mary felt a strange pain in her lower back. Mildred smiled, "It's time. I'll go get Mrs. Johnson."

Mrs. Johnson arrived and took charge. Having six children of her own and birthing most of the children in Prescott, she was an experienced midwife. "I'll need lots of warm water and clean rags." She checked Mary and announced, "You're doing fine." To herself she worried at how small Mary was. Several hours later, a perfect boy screamed his arrival.

Mary laid back and watched while Mrs. Johnson gently bathed him. She swaddled him and laid him by Mary's side. Mary smiled at him and stroked his hand with her finger. He clutched her finger tightly. "My, he's strong."

Mildred came to the bedside grinning, "He'll grow to be a fine lad. What will you name him?"

"I'll call him Brookins Travis for Pa."

"That's a right good name," Mildred agreed.

Note

1. Esther Oakes Carson in her searches for John Heacock, wrote "he seems to have disappeared from all records," which is what several of my cousins and I found.

4.

Meeting Levi Jefferson Oakes

"True love comes quietly, without banners or
flashing lights."
—Eric Segal

The spring of 1853 brought a large log drive with a hoard of lumberjacks to the boarding house. With his rugged good looks, one Levi Oakes caught Mary's eye. His brown hair was parted in the middle, combed to each side, and tucked behind his ears. He had a full beard and mustache, as was the style for woodsmen. His intense brown eyes held her gaze until she blushed. He laughed often and loudly. At supper, Levi entertained the others with stories of his adventures. He was telling of his arrival in Milwaukee: "I walked up to the bell ox (boss) and asked for a job. He asked what I could do, so I told him about my lumbering and cruising days in Maine. That guy hired me on the spot saying the company needed a cruiser in Green Bay. They'd brought a ship of logs down Lake Michigan to be milled. Now the lumber needed to go back to Green Bay. I was hired to help load the deck with lumber and stay on in Green Bay. The boat sailed at dawn. What a trip that was. The worst storm I ever saw blew up. All the lumber washed overboard. None of the crew could stand up on the deck. We put on all the clothes we had and lashed ourselves to the mast to ride out the night. I thought I would freeze to death. Holy cow, how the wind blew. The wind stopped just before dawn, and it was too quiet. When the sun came up, we saw the boat was high and dry on a sandbar. So, boys, that was my introduction to the fine state of Wisconsin." Everyone joined in the laughter. Levi touched her arm as she passed, "Thank you for the fine grub, Miss...." His brown eyes met hers and held them.

Mary blushed, "You're welcome. My name is Mary."

"Mary, I haven't had such a good meal in months."

"Thank you, sir."

"Oh, call me Levi."

Flustered at his sudden familiarity Mary blushed again. "Levi, excuse me, I need to get the dessert from the kitchen."

Levi smiled at her. After dinner he lingered in the dining room when the others left. As Mary gathered up the dirty dishes, he said, "Here, let me help you with those."

"No, thank you. You've been working hard and need a rest."

"Well, may I stay and talk to you?"

Just then Brookins toddled in from the kitchen, "Mama, Mama."

"Who is this?" Levi looked at Mary quizzically.

"This is my son Brookins," Mary beamed.

Levi exclaimed, "I didn't know you were married."

"I'm divorced."

"I'm sorry."

"Don't be. The scoundrel hightailed it two years ago."

After an awkward silence, Levi took his leave, "Well, goodnight." He stayed a few days, always finding ways to talk to Mary. The last night he looked sad. "Mary, I've negotiated with a government agent who says the state wants a survey of the pine in the area around Ashland. The old fur traders' maps showed a huge lake near there. He wants me to determine if it is large enough to float log rafts south."

Mary's eyes widened, "Are you taking the job?"

"Yes, it's too good to pass up."

"Oh, will you be gone long?"

"I'll probably be gone until spring." He paused, blushed, and offered, "I'll miss you."

Mary also blushed, "Brookins and I will miss you, too. We'll look for you come spring."

Over the winter, as Mary knitted, she thought about the fun-loving Levi, wondering where he was. "Why do men always leave?"

Spring 1854

A knock on the back door sent Mary scurrying to answer. The milkman brought fresh milk. "Mornin'. Have you seen? The ice is breakin' up and movin' with a huge log raft comin'? You'll soon have a heap o' lumberjacks."

Mary traded the empty can for the fresh milk. "Thanks, I hadn't seen." Placing the milk can in the icebox on the back stoop, she hurried into the kitchen. "Mildred, the milkman said a huge log raft is comin' down the St. Croix with a heap o' loggers."

Mildred looked up from kneading bread, "Good golly, they're early this year." She sighed, "How did I ever manage without you?"

As soon as her chores were finished, Mary bundled up Brookins, grabbed her coat and they headed out to the point where they could see the St. Croix River. Sure enough, a big raft of logs was coming into view, still too far away to tell who the lumberjacks were. "Come, Brookins, we have work to do. There will be lots of jacks for supper."

At suppertime, the jacks arrived, Levi among them. He just stared at her, seemingly tongue-tied. He wiped his sweaty palms on his pants.

"Hello, stranger," Mary smiled up at him, her face flushed, and her eyes danced. "How was your winter? Did you find the lake by Ashland?"

Levi laughed heartily, "Twasn't any lake—just the finest stand of white pine this side of Maine. They's some punkins."

The visit was brief. Next morning, the crew left. Levi lingered after breakfast until the others had left. "Good-bye, Mary. We have heaps more logs to bring down. I reckon I'll see you in a week or so." He tipped his hat and was gone.

* * *

Somehow Levi managed to be with every log run. At the boarding house, he made himself useful after supper, clearing tables and drying dishes. Mildred observed Mary and Levi with a sly smile. "Why don't you take a cup of tea to the parlor? I'll get Brookins to bed." Both blushed, but evenings in the parlor or on the porch swing became their routine whenever Levi arrived. Mary was curious about this kind man. "Tell me about yourself," she queried.

"There's not much to tell."

"Horse feathers! I've heard you telling stories about being the most American 'cause your great-great-grandpa was the first to come to America," Mary retorted. "Tell me about your family."

"Well, my family says Nathaniel Oak came from Wales or England about 1663 or so. He was a cabin boy on a vessel bound for Boston. Nine miles from land the vessel foundered. All the crew were lost except the cabin boy named Oak. He was a good swimmer and made it ashore. He solemnly promised the Lord that if he would preserve him to get to land, he would never go upon water again. They said he sacredly kept that promise. He would never cross the Charles River to get to Boston and always went around. He often said that while swimming to land, he suffered from hunger more than anything. When he tired, he rested on his back.

"Arriving in his after-home penniless, he bound himself out to earn a living. His master set him to work in a pitch-pine forest to pick up pine knots. He was attacked by a catamount (puma), which he slew with a large knot. His master gave him the bounty the state paid for the pelt. With the money he bought a couple of sheep and let them out to double. These sheep were all the property he began the world with when he came of age and finished his indenture."

He continued, "My family comes from good stock—all healthy, courageous, hard-working, fine citizens. Family stories say my great-grandfather, Captain Jonathan Oaks, fought in the French and Indian War. He was in Quebec when General Wolfe was killed. Grandpa Jonathan was employed to make Wolfe's coffin so his remains could be sent back to England."

"I do believe, that's quite a story. Did you come from Maine?" Mary grinned.

"Yes, I was born August 1, 1825, or thereabouts, near Old Town, Maine. I was the youngest of my ma's five young'uns. She died when I was 12 and my pa remarried. They had another boy, Hartley, who was a great pal. Pa died when I was 16. After that I was sent to my mother's brother, John Carsley III. At Uncle John's, I wasn't brought up, I was kicked up." He shook his head and added, "But I did learn the lumbering business."

"Oh, dear, that's sad. What did you do then?"

Looking up at the ceiling, he paused as if remembering, "Let's see, then, my great uncle, Colonel William Oakes, took me in."

"Oh, was he in the army?"

"He was Colonel of the Maine Militia. Family stories tell of when he lived in Harvard, Massachusetts, he was known for training the local defense band. When I knew him, he had moved to Canaan Plantation in Maine. I really liked his son, Valentine. Uncle William was president of the Board of Trustees at Foxcroft Academy in Dover-Foxcroft, Maine." Levi put his hand over his eyes and reddened, "Colonel William insisted I must go to school. Being 17 years old in the first grade was embarrassing. I asked the teacher if I could recite my lessons after school. She agreed, but I lasted only a year."

Mary smiled, imagining this big man in a school desk. "What did you do then?"

"Oh, I went to up to Aroostook. My brother, Timothy, was there. We worked for Sinclair Lumber Company." Levi chuckled, "I was named foreman and the fellows called me "the Cub" as I was the youngest and smallest lumberjack. I was just 5'9" and weighed 204 pounds." Levi coughed and stretched.

Mary urged, "Go on."

"Timothy and his family left for Wisconsin. He kept in touch and urged me to come west. I hopped on a lumber boat in Buffalo headed for Chicago. I thought I would stay there, but that place is just too swampy. Everyone was talking about the fine piney woods in Wisconsin, so I went on to Green Bay where I hired on as a timber cruiser."

"What's that?"

"That's the fellow who estimates the timber in a given area. Here in northwest Wisconsin that means finding a stream or river with enough timber on both sides to keep a camp working all winter. Trees are cut in the fall and in the winter, logs are skidded over roads on which water had been poured to make ice. This makes moving logs to the river easy; there they are stacked on the frozen river to be floated downstream when the ice goes out in the spring."

"Oh, I remember, that's the story you were telling the first time I saw you."

"You were listening?"

"I couldn't help but hear," Mary teased. "So that's what you've been doing?"

"Yah. Now it's your turn; tell me about you."

"I don't have such a fine tale as yours. I guess Mildred and Brookins are all the family I have now. I haven't heard of my family in Pennsylvania since I married in '48. I do know my parents came from Virginia. I have 11 brothers and sisters. Mildred came out to Wisconsin a few years ago. Brookins is named for my pa. I can't fault him for wanting me married with all those young'uns to feed. I came to Milwaukee on the Great Lakes, too."

"May I ask, what happened to your husband?"

"That scoundrel insisted that I go ahead while he closed up the place in Pennsylvania. He never showed up. Then I got the divorce papers."

"I think he made a great mistake in leaving you," Levi locked eyes with Mary until she blushed and looked down.

"It's just as well. He was too much a dandy," Mary shook her head.

Their times together came to an end a few days later as Levi signed on for the winter to work on the Trade River to the northwest. "Soon we'll be weathered in until the spring thaw," he sadly informed her.

"Will we see you in the spring or is this it?" Mary asked mischievously.

"Oh, you'll see me on the first log run." On impulse, Levi pulled her close and kissed her on the forehead. Just then Brookins toddled in and started pounding on his leg. Levi scooped him up with a laugh. "Goodbye, rug rat, take care of your ma."

Note

1. The story of Nathaniel Oak was told by Levi Jefferson Oakes' sons to their children. Henry Lebbeus Oak wrote in his 1906 book, *Oak, Oaks, Oakes*, that it came from the fly leaf of the family Bible belonging to a grandson of Nathaniel.

5.

Lightning in the North Woods, 1853

"The best lightning rod for your protection is your own spine."

—Ralph Waldo Emerson

The storm was over. The woods were warm and damp with glistening raindrops. The soaking rain made mushrooms pop up. Walking along, she surveyed all her favorite spots, her black eyes darting along the path. Bent over searching for morels, something seemed amiss. Everything was bathed in sunlight, where previously this had been a very shady spot. She straightened and looked. A little further down the trail, an ancient, majestic elm was a charred skeleton against the sky, where lightning had struck. Over the joyful bird songs, there was a faint sound near the tree. She crept forward, her moccasins silent on the spongy, moist ground. The sound was closer now. Was it a person? She inched forward and peered out of a thicket. The giant elm had burned before the torrents of rain had put out the fire. Pools of water still filled low areas. There, near the base of the tree, were three white men with burned clothes. She studied them. She recognized the one closest to her from the lumber camp near her village. She remembered him because of his bright yellow hair, now mostly singed. He didn't move. Again, the sound startled her. The man in the middle moaned and moved ever so slightly in a pool of water. The third man seemed lifeless.

Suddenly the woods were filled with crashing and voices of white men. The Ojibwe woman melted into the hazel brush and watched.

* * *

A lumberjack dashed into the clearing and stopped short. He drew a deep breath and let it out slowly, "Dear God." Then he began to shout, "I found them! I found them! Over here!"

Three men plunged along a deer trail into the clearing and stared. Beneath the burned tree were the blackened remains of tent poles, a kerosene lamp, and three bodies. They rushed forward to examine the men. Two were dead, but Levi was breathing. When they tried to rouse him, he opened his eyes for a second and moaned. The back of his shirt and pants had a burned strip down the middle. The rest of his clothes were only singed.

"Will you look at this?" one exclaimed. "Levi was in this here low spot in a pool of water. That must have saved him. And look at what's left of the kerosene lamp—it must have exploded when lightning struck."

The leader of the search party knelt beside Levi and carefully pulled up the wet torn shirt. He shuddered at what he saw. Lightning had ripped a furrow down Levi's spine. The burned flesh was black and seared. The leader stood up and took charge, "We have to make a stretcher."

The woodsmen quickly set to work chopping nearby poplar saplings. They bound them together with rope from a pack. The leader nodded his approval at the stretcher.

The men rolled the two dead lumberjacks out of the way and placed the stretcher next to Levi's right side. They all knelt on his left, put their arms under him, gently eased him onto the stretcher, and tied him on.

The leader directed, "Let's make haste and get Levi back to camp. Daniel and Seth, you go ahead to clear the trail. Albert and I will carry him a ways Then we can trade places. We'll send someone back for the bodies."

They were up the St. Croix River in northwest Wisconsin about 2 miles from base camp.

The timber cruisers had left a week ago and were due back on Wednesday. When they didn't return, the bell ox sent out a search party.

* * *

Behind them the Ojibwe woman emerged from hiding and surveyed the place. She checked the remaining two men. Yes, they were dead. She touched the blond man's hair. "Is he a ghost?" she thought. White men puzzled her: Why do they cut so many trees? Why does their camp have no women or children? The people in her village were friendly with the white men in the camp. Some of the young braves hung around the camp and learned some English. They traded wild rice for flour, tobacco, and cloth. In the past she had been called to care for sick or injured lumberjacks. She mused, "They'll come get me for this one." She gathered the medicinal plants and bark she would need.

6.

Levi's Recovery

"An injury is not just a process of recovery; it's a process of discovery."

—Conor McGregor

Samuel, crossing the dingle—the alley between the men's camp and mess hall—saw Albert coming up the trail. Samuel cupped his hands around his mouth and shouted, "They're back!"

Men came running.

"Careful, he's hurt real bad," Ebenezer warned. "He was struck by lightning. Charley and Frank are dead."

Daniel and Seth carried the stretcher to the men's camp, a long low building of the "State of Maine" type, about 24 feet by 36 feet with 3-foot side walls. Along the side walls, were beds made of balsam boughs covered with heavy quilts. The lumberjacks slept with their heads against the outside walls. Each jack had a turkey, a grain sack with his personal belongings.

One jack ran ahead and grabbed up his blankets and turkey and directed, "Here. He can have my place next to the fire. I'll take Levi's bed over in the corner."

In the center of the building, a fire crackled on the caboose, an elevated platform of packed dirt. Above the caboose was a hole cut in the shake roof with a mud and stick chimney. A water barrel and washbasin, a grindstone and stacks of firewood stood at one end.

"Gentle like, now," commanded Jacob, the bell ox, as they rolled Levi onto the balsam bough bed. "Well, boys, we'd better get those wet clothes off and see how bad he is."

Levi still had not regained consciousness. They cut off his clothes and rolled him over. The tough woodsmen gasped and fell silent. A blackened, seared furrow ran across his spine from the left shoulder to the right hip. Not sure what to do, they covered him with quilts.

Loggers had two common remedies: Wonder Worker and Balsam Myrrh. Wonder Worker was a liniment used on broken legs and toothaches. Balsam Myrrh was a woods treatment used for split hands. Hot balsam pitch was run into the wound and lighted with a match. They said this allowed the wound to heal with no scar. Neither of these seemed helpful.

Jacob stepped outside and called to an adolescent Ojibwe boy, "Injun, go get medicine woman."

The boy nodded and took a few steps, then turned to Jacob, pointing, "She here." Up the trail came Nokomis, wearing a buckskin dress and moccasins, both beaded with flowers, typical of Ojibwe design. Her black hair hung down her back in one long braid. She carried a large basket filled with berries, leaves, roots, and bark.

Jacob looked where the boy pointed, "Good. Bring her here."

The boy beckoned to her. They entered the camp with Jacob. Men stepped back making room. Nokomis set down her full basket and lifted the quilt. She looked at the wound and spoke to the boy in Ojibwe. He turned to Jacob, "Nokomis needs water—hot."

"I'll get it from the kitchen," volunteered Samuel. He quickly returned with the pot of boiling water. Nokomis stirred certain leaves and bark into the pot with a stick. She left it steeping and asked for more hot water—a small pot. Into it she put other leaves from her basket.

Again, she spoke to the boy. He headed to the kitchen and spoke to the clerk, "Nokomis need cloth." The clerk opened the wanigan—a large box with items for sale. He took out a bolt of muslin and tore off a couple of yards and handed it to the boy. Returning with the muslin, he gave it to Nokomis who smiled and nodded as she took the cloth, tore off some strips and dropped them into the larger pot. Next, she took clumps of moss from the basket and dipped them into the brew, then carefully sponged the wound. Fresh moss was soaked in the pot and placed along the wound. The wet strips of cloth were laid over the moss. With the remaining dry cloth, she wrapped his body to hold the wet strips of cloth and moss in place. She covered him with a quilt. Sitting next to him, she cradled his head so she could raise it. Slowly, spoonful by spoonful, she poured the herbal tea into his mouth.

* * *

The camp was a buzz of activity. Four men were sent to retrieve the bodies; two were making pine caskets; and four were digging two graves in a clearing.

"Maybe we should be digging three graves," Albert commented.

"Yeah, it'll be a miracle if Levi survives," replied Samuel, brushing a tear from his eyes.

At 6 p.m., Gabriel's horn called everyone to dinner. What a crew they were. Like Levi, most were Yankees from Maine and northern New York. The usual joking was gone as they ate in silence. Tonight, they missed Levi's hearty laugh. He often teased, "I'm the most American. You know my great-great-grand-pappy came to Massachusetts in 1663." A raucous protest would start an evening of boasting.

Jacob asked, "Anyone know where Timothy is?" Timothy Oakes, Levi's older brother, had come to Wisconsin the year before with his wife and two toddler sons in tow.

One man spoke up, "I heard he's a sod buster down near New Richmond."

"Better send word downriver to see if someone can find him," Jacob replied.

* * *

Nokomis came to the camp each day with a basket of fresh bark, leaves, grasses, and berries to make tea and the brew for fresh dressings on Levi's back. Some days she brought a rabbit to cook a broth. Levi faded in and out of consciousness for some time. Finally, he opened his eyes. "Where am I?" he thought, trying to sit up. "Oh, my back," he moaned, falling back on the bed. Looking around, he realized he was in the camp. Then he remembered the storm, lightning, and terrible fire when the kerosene lamp exploded. By slowly rolling onto his side, he could prop himself up on an elbow.

Nokomis heard his moan and roused. Shaking her head and talking rapidly, she motioned for him to lie still. Movement was painful; he lay down. Hearing the door open he called out, "Who's there?"

Albert hurried over to the bedside. "How ya' doin?"

"Been better. How'd I get here? How are Charley and Frank?"

"Well, some of the jacks carried you in. I hate to tell you; Charley and Frank didn't make it."

Levi was silent with this news. "How long have I been here?"

Albert replied, "Oh, a few weeks."

When they heard Levi was coming around, the men whooped and hollered, smacking their thighs. They came to greet him with the usual banter, "Why you ol' coot, you're just too ornery to die."

Nokomis washed the wound with the brew. This time she did not put on fresh dressings. The Brave told Levi, "Nokomis say you better now. No need her more."

Levi held out his hand to her and spoke to the lad, "Tell her I am plumb glad of her doctorin'."

The two nodded and silently slipped out of camp.

* * *

A week later when Gabriel's horn announced dinner, Levi said to Samuel, "I'll walk to dinner." Slowly with a palsied gait and leaning on the crutches that Samuel had carved, he struggled across the dingle. He couldn't lift his leg, so someone had to lift it over the threshold. He would walk with a palsied gait for the rest of his life.

The next morning the traveling doctor arrived. He came occasionally to check on the lumberjacks. He entered the mess hall asking, "Where's the miracle man I've heard about?"

"He's still in the sack, the lazy bum," a jack replied.

The doctor headed to the camp, "Mornin' Levi. How are you?" He extended his hand and shook Levi's, which he noted with a frown, had lost its strong grip.

"I've been better," Levi grinned.

"Let's have a look at that back."

Levi sat up and removed his shirt and vest. The doctor whistled softly as he observed the healed furrow across Levi's spine. "Well, the medicine woman did a fine job. I do remember you were the strongest man in the county. Time will tell how your strength returns. Good luck to you." He shook hands and left.

* * *

A couple of weeks later, a tall man came from the south trail, pausing to watch Levi struggle across the dingle. He broke into a run, shouting "Levi! Mon Dieu, Comment vas-tu?"

Levi looked up and smiled at his brother, "Salut, Timothy. Je ne vais pas tres bien." The brothers often peppered their conversation with French learned from their French-Canadian Grandma Lydia who had never learned English.

Timothy held Levi by the shoulders at arm's length. He studied his brother closely. He stared and exclaimed, "What happened to your eyes?"

"My eyes? What's wrong with them?"

"Why they're crystal blue!"

"Horse feathers! You ol' jokester."

"No, they are, I swear."

Before the accident Levi's eyes had been brown, but now were blue. The brothers made their way to the mess hall, where they were greeted with shouts, whistles, and clapping. That evening, Timothy turned to Levi, "There's good land with meadows, oak stands, and a clear creek next to mine. Come back with me."

Levi looked at his brother and sighed. Farming may be alright. His lumbering days were over. He'd never again hike the woods with this bum limb. Over the next two years he went many times to the hospital in Hudson for treatment.

Note

1. Family lore tells the story of Levi's eyes turning blue; however, I could not find any reference to such a condition. Dr. Michael Stanko, Ophthalmologist, said the iris would not change color, but if the lightening touched the surface of the eye, the cornea would be cloudy and may appear bluish.

7.

Home in Richmond Township

"The country is beautiful, adorned with oak woods and prairies broken by rivers and lakes swarming with fish; and in addition, one of the healthiest areas in America."

—Gustoph Unoniur, Letter from Wisconsin, 1841

When Levi was strong enough to travel, he and Timothy hopped on a keelboat down the St. Croix to Hudson. There they purchased a wagon and an ox team and a load of lumber, which they drove the 15 miles to Timothy's land on the south side of Richmond township. Timothy had built a small cabin where his wife, Angelina, and two young sons, Franklin and Princeton, were waiting for them.

Frank heard them first. He pushed open the wooden door yelling, "Papa, Papa!" He ran down the lane right into Timothy's arms. Laughing, Timothy lifted him up and swung him to the top of the lumber. As they reached the cabin, Angelina stood smiling with Prince in her arms. Timothy hurried to embrace her.

"How's he doing?" Angelina inquired, nodding toward Levi sitting on the wagon box.

"You'll see." Timothy took Prince and tossed him in the air to his squeals of laughter.

Levi climbed slowly down from the wagon and, with shaking legs, made his way to Angelina. He grasped her hand and shook it, "Mighty glad to be here."

"Welcome, Levi. I'm plumb tickled to see ya." Angelina noted that his handshake was weak, but his laugh was still hearty.

While Angelina rustled up a snug supper of chicken fixins, eggs, and even slapjacks, the men unhitched the oxen and staked them out in the meadow by Paper Jack Creek. After supper, they talked of the land.

Timothy enthused, "You'll not be sorry you came. This is the best gol' darn land anywhere. Why, plants just pop out of the ground. With only one turn of the plow, you can plant sod corn this year. By Jove, you can stand and watch it grow. There'll be time in the fall to work the ground again and till it for next year's wheat."

The next morning, Levi and Timothy walked around the 120 acres, just north of Timothy's claim, across Paper Jack Creek. The morning dew sparkled in the sunshine. From a high spot, they surveyed the landscape—prairie grass with lots of clover rolled in the wind like pink ocean waves. The prairie was punctuated by magnificent woodlands of oaks, maples, butternuts, elms, and fields where settlers had plowed the sod and planted wheat, oats, barley, rye, and corn.

Timothy swept his arm in a circle. "This is the richest farmland in the county." He kicked a clod of grass to expose the dirt and stooped to pick up a handful of the rich black loam. "Just look—black gold. It'll grow anything. It's a good time to buy. The government agent is drawing up contracts. There's about 600 people in the county now and it's growing fast."

The brothers stood quietly admiring the view. Timothy, although about four years older, looked younger. He was shorter but stood straighter. His ruddy complexion belied long hours in the sun. Levi, still recovering, was stooped and pale. But no mistake—they were brothers with the same short noses and broad foreheads. Timothy wore blue denim bib overalls with a red flannel shirt, typical of farmers. Levi still had on heavy canvas pants and a blue plaid shirt of nor' woodsmen.

Levi breathed deeply, "Just smell the clover." He pointed toward the distant St. Croix River. "Must be hundreds of acres of clover over yonder."

"Ya betcha. Folks call it Clover City."

"You say no one has claimed these 120 acres?" Levi responded.

"That's right. Just look at this prairie. All it needs is a plow and oxen."

The acreage north of Timothy's was ideal: the north part sloped up the hill toward town with a stand of about forty acres of ancient oaks each wide as a molasses barrel and 40-feet tall. The south side had rolling prairie that would be easily plowed.

The brothers made the trip to the land office in Hudson and returned with papers for a 30- year note for the property. Levi chose a house site on the north side of Paper Jack Creek within sight of Timothy's cabin.

The brothers worked together digging a well and outhouse hole, moving rocks from the hillside for the foundation and building of the two-story frame house. The first floor had three rooms: a kitchen, the other room (parlor), and a small bedroom. The second floor had two bedrooms.

As he worked, Levi thought about his trips to Prescott and Mary. He admired her grit to travel alone to the frontier and make a life for herself and her son. She was such a pretty little thing, her dark brown eyes seemed to dance in her delicate face; her long dark hair was always tidy in a bun at the nape of her neck; and her waist was tiny. He was certain he could put his hands completely around that waist and he longed to do so. Whenever there had been a chance to float a log raft downriver, he had volunteered. Last spring Mary seemed as happy to see him as he was her. In his mind, he replayed that visit:

"Hello, stranger," Mary smiled up at him, her face flushed and her eyes dancing. "How was your winter? Did you find the lake by Ashland?"

"No lake—just the finest stand of white pine this side of Maine. They's some punkins," Levi laughed heartily. He was often tongue-tied in her presence. He found his heart pounding and his palms sweaty. Did she feel it, too? The last time he was there, in May of '54, he had kissed her forehead when he said goodbye. That was almost a year ago.

* * *

When the last nail was pounded on the house, Levi ever so casually announced at supper, "I reckon I'll head down to Prescott. I heard there's a new warehouse where I could get a cookstove. Do you want me to bring anything for you?"

Both Timothy and Angelina pounced on his words. "Ho, Ho!" they said together.

"What?" Levi looked at them innocently.

"Do tell. Levi's goin' a courtin'!" Angelina exclaimed.

He blushed and shrugged.

"What if she gives you the mitten?" Timothy teased and winked at Angelina.

Levi hadn't considered that Mary might refuse his proposal. He got up and walked out across the yard to the necessary.

8.

Courtin'

"Courtship consists in a number of quiet attentions, not so pointed as to alarm, nor so vague as not to be understood."
—Laurence Sterne

Mary was hanging out the wash in the back yard. Brookins, now four years old, was handing the metal clothes pins to her. She glanced up to see a man staggering toward them on crutches. She frowned. "Is he drunk?" she thought.

The man smiled broadly and waved, "Mary!"

Mary stared. The voice was familiar. "Levi?" she asked hesitantly.

His cheerful laugh boomed, "Yes, it's me."

Brookins ran to him, "Levi, Levi."

Levi patted the boy on the head and continued to walk to Mary. They just looked at each other, both overcome with sudden shyness. Finally, Mary asked, "What happened to your limb?" It was considered impolite to call it a leg.

"I was struck by lightning up north. There's a furrow down my back. When it mended, my limbs didn't work so good. Other than that, I'm fine. I'm right lucky to be alive. My silk vest (undershirt) and being in a pool of water saved me."

Mary was stunned. "Land sakes! What brings you to town?"

"I need some fixin's for my house."

"Your house?" Mary was surprised.

"Yes. This bum limb will keep me from cruisin' so I staked a claim next to Timothy near New Richmond. We just finished building my house. Now I need a cook stove."

"There's a new mercantile down by the docks. Last week I saw a cook stove there," Mary offered.

"Good. Will you go with me tomorrow?"

"Yes, if you want." Mary blushed.

"I do."

Mary and Levi sat after supper talking. Levi considered asking for her hand, but then cautioned himself, "wait until tomorrow and see how it goes". Out loud, he said, "Those adenoids bothering you?" He had noticed that Mary's breathing was more difficult than he had remembered.

"Yes, it seems they fill up my whole nose. Sometimes it's worse. I don't know why my adenoids must keep growing. Mildred says usually they disappear once you're grown up." That night, Mary had to breathe through her mouth, making her speech come in gasps. Little did they know just how much worse they would become.

The next evening as they lingered in the parlor, Levi took a deep breath, reached for Mary's hand, and said, "Mary, I'd be mighty proud if you'd consent to marry me."

Mary squealed with delight, "Oh, Levi, that would make me so happy." He picked her up, his large hands encircling her tiny waist and spun around the room. They were laughing when Mary shouted, "Stop! Stop!"

The commotion brought Mildred running, "Lan' sakes, have you lost your minds?"

Levi stopped and put Mary down. Catching his breath and drawing himself up tall, he laughed, "Madam, your dear sister has just consented to be my wife." He turned to Mary, and both stifled their laughter.

"Do tell. I reckoned you didn't come just for a cook stove. Come, sit, and spill the beans. I want to know all your plans," Mildred chuckled.

"Plans? Why, we don't have any," Mary blurted out.

Mildred nodded, asserting, "Seems to me you ought to get married here by the Justice of the Peace and go back with Levi. It's a long trip and who knows when the travelin' preacher will come through."

Levi's eyes danced, "That sounds good, 'cause I need to get back to plowin' and buildin' a barn. What do you think, Mary?"

"Suits me," Mary smiled up at him and reached for his hand. "We can have a proper ceremony whenever the preacher gets there."

The next morning when Brookins awakened, Mary told him, "Levi's going to be your pa. As soon as we pack, we'll go with him up north to his home."

Brookins studied her face with large round eyes. "Can I bring my new slingshot?"

"Of course," Mary scooped him up in a big bear hug.

9.

Wedding

"Being deeply loved by someone gives you strength While loving someone deeply gives you courage."

—Lao Tzu

When Mary, Levi, and Brookins arrived at the farmstead, Timothy and Angelina greeted them warmly. Frank and Prince were thrilled to have a new playmate. The two women set about making the house livable.

Angelina greeted Mary, "I'm so happy you're here. It gets lonely without any women folk."

"Did you come from Maine, too?" Mary asked.

"Oh, yes. I came from Aroostook County."

"Do you have family there?" Mary inquired.

"Yes—four sisters and two brothers. My brother, Isaac, wrote that he might come out to Wisconsin. What about you?" Angelina sat down and paused as she filled a tick with chicken feathers. She was pregnant, due soon, and tired more easily.

"I was born in Luzerne County, Pennsylvania. Most of my family is still in that area, but I've lost touch. I don't know about my family except for my sister Mildred in Prescott."

"We'll just have to stick together out here on the frontier," Angelina replied.

* * *

A few weeks later, Levi returned from the lumber mill with news. "Mary, I saw Paper Jack, the newspaper boy, over near the river. He said he saw Preacher Jones out near Hudson, and he'll be here next week. I told him if he sees Preacher Jones to tell him we need him here."

"That's wonderful," Mary replied.

Levi swooped her up and spun her around. "Sure, you really want a ceremony? There's time to back out," he teased.

"Levi Jefferson Oakes, you scoundrel. Put me down," Mary feigned annoyance. Then she laughed, "Oh, no, you're not getting off the hook that easy. Do put me down, there's work to do. I want to go tell Angelina."

He put her down. Untying her apron, she hung it on a peg, took her bonnet, and headed outside where Brookins was playing in the dirt. She reached for his hand, "Come, we're going to see Frank and Prince." They hurried down the lane to the steppingstones across Paper Jack Creek and up the hill to see Angelina and her boys.

Smiling to himself, Levi watched them go. "What a lucky man I am."

* * *

The week was filled with preparations. Surveying the lovely prairie grass on the south side of the house, Levi noted, "I'll just take the scythe to that grass, and we'll have a right good place for the wedding. There are some boards in the shed to make a couple of tables and some benches."

Mary nodded in agreement. "June is a lovely month, isn't it? I'm glad we can be outside."

Angelina arrived with Frank and Prince. "Good mornin'. Is this the wedding chapel?"

"Sure is," Mary responded. She fetched a blanket and spread it on the grass. The women sat down while the boys played in the grass.

"Mary, what are you going to wear?"

"I have a navy voile dress in my trunk."

"Oh, I want to see it."

"Come, it's in the house." The small trunk in the corner of the parlor had a flat top; pine stays were nailed over boards and heavy cowhide straps fastened it. Mary unbuckled the straps and opened the trunk. She lifted the dress wrapped in muslin and laid it on the settee. Carefully she unwrapped it and held it for Angelina to see.

"It's lovely," Angelina smiled.

Mary sat down on a chair and ran her fingers over the lace suddenly remembering the last time she wore it. She stared into space.

"Mary? Mary? Are you alright?"

Startled out of her reverie, Mary sighed, "Yeah, I was thinking of the last time I wore this dress. I was standing on the pier in Milwaukee waiting for that no-good husband who was busy filing for divorce."

"Oh, I'm so sorry. This will be a happier time. Levi adores you and brags about you all the time," Angelina patted Mary's hand.

"It's alright. It was good he left. I see that Levi is a good man." Mary gathered up the dress, shook it to remove wrinkles and hung it on a peg.

The women returned to the blanket. "I expect the neighbors will bring their favorite dishes, as they usually do for gatherings." Angelina counted on her fingers: "Mrs. Smith always brings deviled eggs; Mrs. Taylor brings milk for her passel of kids; Mrs. Johansson makes the best pies around; Mrs. Foster bakes rolls; and Mrs. Russell outdoes herself with chicken and dumplings. I have peas and young carrots in the garden."

"We don't have much yet. We brought sacks of rice, beans, flour, and cornmeal from Prescott. And prunes—they'll do nicely for wedding cake. I'll make baked beans and Jonnie cake," Mary added.

"We'll have to bake cookies for the shivaree," Angelina exclaimed.

"What's that?"

"The shivaree? It's the pronunciation for the French Chiavari and the custom here. All the neighbors gather to hassle the newlyweds. They come after you have hopefully gone to bed so they may embarrass you in your night clothes. They sing and make a ruckus on tin kettles, until you let them in and give treats."

"Oh, my, we called that horning back home," Mary nodded.

"We did, too, in Maine. I remember we were awakened from a dead sleep by the greatest din and shouting. There was so much noise it was a sin to Moses!" Angelina laughed.

Mary glanced skyward. The sun was straight overhead. "Goodness, it's time for dinner."

"So, it is. We must be getting home. Come Frank." Angelina picked up Prince and waved goodbye.

Late on Tuesday afternoon a horseman rode up to the house. Levi went to meet him. "Greetings, stranger."

"I'm Reverend Jones. I hear you want me to perform a wedding."

"Ya betcha." Levi shook his hand. "Come in, you're just in time for supper."

After supper, Reverend Jones smiled. "Thank you, Mrs. Oakes, that was just what I needed."

"It wasn't much," Mary apologized.

"It really hit the spot. Now let's settle on a time. I reckon Thursday about 11 o'clock is good. It gives time for neighbors to be notified. Is someone giving you away?"

Mary snorted, "Posh! There's only me."

Brookins piped up, "I'll give her."

Everyone laughed. "All right, young man," Reverend Jones replied and shook Brookins' hand.

Thursday dawned sunny and warm. Mary went to the woods above the house and picked wildflowers. She returned and plopped them in a bucket of water and set them on the table spread with a calico cloth. After chores, Mary filled a basin with hot water from the reservoir on the cook stove. She washed up and went upstairs to dress.

Levi came in from the barn and washed up. He put on his "go-to-meetin'" black trousers and white shirt. The stiffly starched collar was a challenge for his large, calloused hands. "Mary, can you do these gol' darn buttons?"

"Of course, silly." Her tiny fingers deftly buttoned the collar to the shirt. Then she placed the gold collar pin. His black jacket had velvet piping around the collar and lapels. He slipped it on and stood awkwardly in the unaccustomed finery. "Mr. Oakes, you are very handsome," Mary beamed.

"No match for my beautiful bride," Levi responded. Hearing wagons and laughter, they went to greet their guests.

10.

Life at Oakes Grove

"We built a house, then after building the house, we enter into it, and we never leave."

—Fredrick Lindemann

The back-bending work to turn the claims into farms, occupied the brothers during the spring through the fall of 1855. In northern Wisconsin in summer, sunrise came about 4 a.m. and sunset was at 9:30 p.m. Levi was out of the house when the rooster crowed. When he came in for dinner about noon, he would often flop down on the daybed in the corner for a quick snooze.

The sandstone cliffs on the east side of Levi's property sheltered a ravine along the north side of Paper Jack Creek. Levi and Timothy quarried rocks there for the foundations of their buildings. Levi chipped out a piece from a vein along the excavation. Holding it up, he called to Timothy, "Look at this."

Timothy rose from where he was digging and walked over to examine it. "Well, what do you know? This is first rate limestone. We'd better build a kiln. We'll get plenty of quick lime."

Drawing on memory from Aroostook, Maine, and many discussions, the brothers built the kiln into the hillside. The kiln produced top-quality quicklime. It was mixed with sand and water for mortar to hold foundation rocks together.

Sandstone rocks were loaded on the ox wagon and carried to the building sites for the foundations of out buildings. Levi staked out foundations about 200-500 feet apart. "One can't be too careful. That ought to be far enough to prevent the spread of fire. I never want to be in another fire," Levi explained. He shuddered, remembering the lightning strike, the kerosene lantern exploding, and the tent in flames.

He built the horse barn into the bank of a hill near the creek. The rock and mortar walls were 18 inches thick and about 7 feet high. Only the roof and door were timber.

Word spread and soon the brothers were providing quick lime and rocks for the whole village—houses, shops, stables, and schools.

Meanwhile, Mary and Brookins worked on the garden to provide potatoes, carrots, onions, and rutabagas for winter. In the summer they enjoyed pie plant (rhubarb), fresh peas, green beans, spinach, and squash. The surrounding woods provided wild blueberries, raspberries, blackberries, strawberries, and honey. Sometimes at the end of the day, Mary was too tired to climb the stairs to the bedroom. She just lay down on the daybed to sleep.

* * *

By the spring of 1856, the brothers each had several buildings. In early June, Mary came to see the progress with infant Albion (born May 20) in her arms and Brookins running along beside her. Levi clucked the baby under the chin and then took Mary's arm to guide her. "Just look at them," he pointed out each building. "There's the hay barn that will get filled this summer; over there the cows will be cool in summer and warm in winter. I just finished the chicken coop here near the garden. Is that alright for you?"

"Of course," Mary replied. "Brookins is old enough to gather eggs."

Each year they added something—a corncrib, granary, pig barn, smoke house, bee house, and machine shed.

* * *

One day in late March 1857, Mary had just put Albion down for a nap and stepped outside. Looking skyward at the sound, Mary saw the "V" of Canada Geese flapping north, their wild calls surely the harbinger of spring. She ran to the barn where Levi was teaching Brookins to sharpen a hoe on the grinding wheel. "Come quickly," she shouted. Levi and Brookins dropped the hoe and ran outside. "See, spring is coming," Mary announced. They watched the geese until they were out of sight.

Levi swooped Mary up and swung her around. They laughed with joy that the long, cold winter was over. Soon they could gather dandelion greens and fiddleheads for dinner.

During 1859-60, war was brewing and became the Civil War, 1860-65. Wisconsin, not being a slave state, sided with the Union. Much of the vast reserve of forest was cut to provide lumber for the Union war effort. Wisconsin sent many young men. In her heart, Mary was glad that her husband was too old and her sons too young to go to war.

Mary was hoeing the garden with help from Silas. Baby Charles, born August 20, 1862, was asleep in a cart at the edge of the garden. The older boys, Albion and Brookins, had gone to town with Levi. They had left early in the morning to get supplies with the wagon and ox team. Ox teams were practical on the frontier. Although slower than horses, they were not as excitable and were better for logging. They took less work. A yoke could be carved from a log, which was less expensive than the leather needed for harnesses and reins. If an ox broke a leg, it could be used for meat while a horse was a total loss. It was thought that only soldiers and post riders needed horses for fast travel.

Mary heard the wagon rattling up the lane. Silas dropped his hoe and ran toward the wagon shouting, "Look what Pa has."

Mary stood up and looked. A pair of bay horses was pulling the wagon. Tom and Jack, the oxen, were tied behind the wagon. Levi drove the team to the barn with Mary following behind pulling the cart with Charles.

"Whoa," Levi called to the horses. He tied the reins to the front of the wagon and jumped down. "What do you think, Ma?"

"Where did you get them?" Mary asked.

"I bought them for $75. A fella was moving here from down river. He says these Belgium draft horses will work circles around ol' Tom and Jack."

"Well, I never," Mary shook her head.

"Won't it be nice to have the first horses in New Richmond?"

Mary just laughed. Levi was full of surprises. Why just a year ago, he had come home with the strangest birds she had ever seen. Peacocks. In a few years they had a flock. The eggs were tasty, as was the meat. Levi enjoyed the birds' antics. They lived in the hay barn. The cocks would fly to the roof and strut along the ridge, fanning their iridescent tails and calling in their loud, raucous voices, much to the amusement of the family and visitors. When the males molted, the boys picked up the long tail plumes to play.

"Bring some feathers to the house," Mary called. "I'll have a nice bouquet."

11.

Babies, Babies, Babies

"A new baby is like the beginning of all things—wonder, hope, a dream of possibilities."
—Edna J. Le Shan

Albion was born May 20, 1856. Mary found this second pregnancy easier. Her sister-in-law, Angelina, encouraged her and gave advice. Angelina was four years older than Mary and had three children. Angelina came to help Mary, bringing one-year-old Lewis. Frank, seven years old, and Prince, four years old, stayed at home to help their father.

"Oh, just listen to that lusty cry. He's got good lungs, Mary, and he's hungry," Angelina remarked as she brought a cup of tea to Mary. She picked up the baby from his cradle and took him to Mary for nursing.

The next year, Mary returned the favor when Angelina had her fourth baby. Mary was assisting when the midwife announced, "It's a girl."

"Really?" Angelina leaned on her elbows to look. She laughed, "I can't believe it after all these boys." They named her Della.

The families joked that it was Mary's turn for a baby. Silas arrived October 18, 1858.

"Another fine boy," Levi announced. "I'll have lots of help soon with Brookins already a good field hand."

Over the next few years, Angelina birthed three children: John (1859), George (1861), and Ida (1863). The families joked that it certainly was Mary's turn to have another child. November 27, 1862, Charles Andrew was born. Angelina and Mary were both pregnant in 1866. Angelina had Leon in April and Mary had William was born August 2, 1866. She had tired so easily and her gasping breath was more frequent towards the end of this last pregnancy. The adenoids were protruding down her nostrils. She had tried hot mustard plasters, poultices of warm water and herbs, and she drank different herbal teas, but nothing helped. Then the adenoids hardened and protruded like fingernails. Levi came to her aid, "Here, Mary, I'll just trim them back." He took out his pen knife to gently trim them.

1870

In July, Mary began to suspect that there were twins growing under her heart. She confided in Angelina, "I'm so big, and with all the kickin' and movin', it must be twins.

"Land sakes alive, that would be exciting." Angelina replied.

In the night September 21, Mary awakened to contractions. She woke Levi, "I think you'd better get Angelina."

Levi aroused Brookins and Albion, "Ma's time has come. Brookins, go get Angelina. Albion, bring in more wood and we'll get the fire going." Levi grabbed a bucket and went to the well for water. He filled the copper reservoir on the stove, knowing Angelina would want warm water.

Angelina arrived and gave orders, "Get some flannels from the cupboard. Bring a kettle of hot water and a basin to the bedroom." By now all the boys were awake. "Silas, take Charles and William to my house and tuck them in with my boys."

At daybreak on September 22, Angelina delivered a boy that did not gasp for breath. She held him up and smacked him on the butt; there was no response. She tied and cut the umbilical cord, wrapped him in a flannel blanket and handed him to Levi, "Rub his back and open his mouth. I think there is another one coming."

No amount of rubbing aroused the infant to gasp and breathe. He was the first one of the family to be buried in the plot that Levi had just purchased in the new City Cemetery of New Richmond.

Angelina delivered the second boy, who immediately gasped and cried. Angelina smiled, "That's more like it."

Levi got the spring scale to weigh him. The baby was laid on a square of flannel and the opposite corners tied together. The tied ends were put on the hook and the scale lifted so the baby in the blanket weighted the scale. "Two pounds," Levi announced. He was frightened to hold such a wee baby.

They named him Fredrick Moses. He was placed in a small grape basket lined with a piece of sheepskin covered with a flannel blanket. The basket was placed on the open oven door to keep him warm. The older boys were given the task of keeping the fire going around the clock. Mary moved down to the daybed so she could nurse the baby every hour. He prospered and grew, but he was always smaller than his brothers. As an adult he was about five and half feet tall, of slight build.

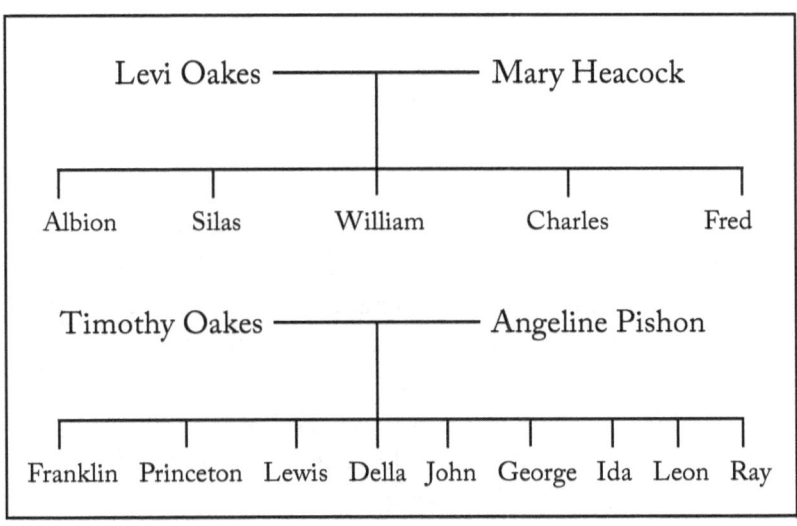

Fig. 2 Babies of Mary and Angelina

12

Northern Lights 1859

"I have been as sincere a worshipper of Aurora as the Greeks."

—Henry David Thoreau

Mary awoke with a start. The bedroom was flooded with a bright rosy light. Thinking she had overslept, she quickly arose and dressed. Her moving about the room awakened Levi. He leaped up exclaiming, "Goodness to Betsy, it must be late. What a sunrise."

"Yes, isn't it something? I'll get the fire started," Mary replied. She descended to the kitchen. Opening the firebox on the cook stove, she thought, "How odd, there's still a lot of coals." The embers flamed as she blew on them. Quickly she started adding thin pieces of kindling.

Levi came down the stairs as the grandfather clock in the parlor struck two. Startled, they stared at each other. "That old clock's gone haywire," Mary laughed.

Levi pulled on the leather cord attached to his overalls and out came the pocket watch. He pushed the button on the top and the cover popped open. It, too, was at 2 o'clock. Puzzled, they hurried out the back door. Although the sky appeared as dawn, it was crimson with brilliant green streaks. "Northern lights," Levi announced. "I've never seen them so bright." They stood gazing heavenward in awe. Sometimes the streaking green lights were accompanied with flashes of white light that made a crackling sound.

"Ma, Pa, what's going on?" Brookins cried as he ran down the steps.

"Come watch. It's northern lights," Mary greeted him.

"Look! Did you see that?" Brookins shouted. The green streaks danced up the ever- reddening sky, sometimes widening, sometimes shrinking. It was like a great symphony. They turned their faces up and their mouths were agape in wonder. Birds were chirping their dawn chorus and the cows mooed in the barn.

Albion toddled out. "Is it morning?"

Mary scooped him up. "No, it's the northern lights."

"What makes them?" Brookins wanted to know.

"Nobody really knows," Levi offered. "I've heard its volcanoes on the other side of the world; while some say they're spirits from God's own hand."

"No matter what, they're mighty handsome, but rather spooky," Brookins retorted.

"So they are," Mary agreed.

"I want to go to bed," Albion whined.

"That's a right good idea," Mary answered. She turned and walked to the house.

From across Paper Jack Creek, they heard Timothy shout. Levi and Brookins ran down the hill, skipped across the creek on the steppingstones they'd laid. Timothy, Frank, Prince, and Lewis were also awed by the display. Everyone talked at once exclaiming over the strange lights. "It's bright as day, but I reckon we'd better get some sleep," Timothy announced. "Come on boys."

"Goodnight, we'll jabber in the morning. Maybe tomorrow's paper will tell us more," Levi answered.

* * *

The morning paper told of the fantastic light display, but not much else. A few days later, Levi returned from town with news. The aurora borealis was seen around the world and all the way to Cuba. "A fellow in London, a Richard Carrington, saw fireballs on the sun in his telescope. The flashes of light caused telegraph lines to fail," he reported. "They're calling it the Carrington Effect. Why, in Washington, D.C., arcs of fire jumped from the machines and burned the paper. In Boston, after unplugging the batteries, they could still send messages with celestial electricity. Even the telegraph lines they're building across Nebraska Territory sparked and started fires."

"I do declare, that seems unbelievable," Mary retorted. "I hope it doesn't happen again."

"Nah, they say it's a freak thing. It happens only once in a blue moon," Levi assured her. He took a deep breath. "What smells so good?"

"There's a cake in the oven and I just put the bread to spring."

"I have to plow the back field and then I'll be back for a piece of cake to see if it's fit to eat," Levi teased.

"Oh, go on with you," Mary playfully slapped his arm.

13.

Revival

"Oh! Men and brethren what would this heart feel if I could but believe that some of you would go home and pray for revival."

—Charles Spurgeon

It was a hot, muggy June afternoon when a buggy with two men from town arrived. Mary recognized them from the Methodist group that met on Sundays in different homes. She went out to greet them.

"Howdy, Ma'am," one said. "Is Levi around?"

"He's out in the field. I'll send one of the boys to get him. Come, sit in the shade. I'll get some sassafras tea and cookies."

"Thank you," both said. They tied the horse to the hitching post.

Levi hurried up smiling, "What brings you out here on such a hot day?"

"Well, there's a preacher comin' up this way lookin' for a place for a camp meetin'. We are wonderin' if we might use your grove?" asked Lucas, the taller one.

"Of course. That will give us a chance to visit with our neighbors. When do you think the preacher will come?"

"We'll send word back that we have a place, so I expect it will be in about three weeks," Lucas replied.

"People can get water from our well. It's got mighty sweet water. Maybe I'd better get my boys to dig a couple of necessaries," Levi grinned.

They laughed and agreed.

A few weeks later, the wagons came rolling into Oakes Grove from miles around.

Preacher Jones arrived and began directing activities. They would have a center circle of wagons and chairs. "Who plays the fiddle or harmonica?" Preacher Jones inquired. "We'll want music tonight."

Everyone was busy setting up tents, as they would stay three or four days. Several fire pits were scraped out and ringed with rocks. The women were busy talking as they prepared the evening meal. At night, the grove was lit by fires built on small platforms about 3 feet off the ground and covered with clay. These elevated fires provided light. There was also a speaker's platform and benches.

After dinner Preacher Jones called people to gather around. He stood on the speaker's platform, towering above the crowd. With bellowing voice and flailing arms, he began, "Sinners, come confess your sins. Jesus is waiting. Come right down here by me and confess your sins. I know there are sinners out there. All God wants is for you to come and confess. Repent and be saved."

Many got religion that night. Preacher Jones tongue-lashed the Devil. "You've got to sing and shout to keep that Devil out. Come on, get out those fiddles and harmonicas, we're goin' sing."

Old fiddle players and others who played harmonicas and Jew's harps joined him. Everyone joined in with a lusty round:

Because they sing and shout the best
The devil hates the Methodist.

The Oakes families of Levi and Timothy sat together. Levi's sons: Brookins (13), Albion (8), and Silas (4) sat by Leiv. Beside Timothy sat his sons: Frank (15), Prince (12), Lewis (9), and John (5). The older boys sat quietly, but the younger ones kept giggling until Levi reached over and boxed Albion and Silas's ears. Mary held Charles (two-weeks old) and Angelina held Ida (1) while Della (7) leaned against her.

Preacher Jones announced, "Tomorrow we'll have a baptism for all of those who choose to come to the Lord." Then he offered a benediction and set morning prayers for 6 a.m.

Levi picked up sleeping Charles while Brookins took cranky, sleepy Silas. Mary smiled, "It's nice to have a real preacher, and tomorrow we'll get all the boys baptized."

Levi nodded.

The next evening, everyone was in a jovial mood. There had been many baptisms and people felt uplifted. Fires were built, and people gathered to talk. Silas was sitting on Levi's lap, "Pa, tell the story about how Paper Jack Creek got its name."

Levi chuckled, "Oh, that's quite a tale. One story is that a peddler named Jack would buy stacks of newspapers over in Hudson and ramble through the countryside selling them, so people called him Paper Jack. He always got to our place at dinnertime so he could enjoy Ma's good cookin'. One spring when the creek was flooding from the melting snow, he got to the other side of the creek at about dark. He thought he could wade across at the usual place, but the water was deep and fast. He lost his footing. To keep from being swept away, he took off his pack of papers and let it go. Papers were everywhere. Ever since we've all called it Paper Jack Creek."

14.

Indian Scare, 1862

"My sense of right would lead me to give Indians as fair and full a trial as white men."
—Reverend Stephen Riggs, 1862

Levi turned toward the clatter of hoof beats. A large bay horse and rider hell bent for leather raced up the maple-lined lane. An early frost had turned the trees scarlet. The leaves trembled in the late August sunshine. The rider, reining in his horse, came to stop by Levi who noticed the young man was a stranger in these parts.

"The Indians are coming," he shouted. "Bring your guns and family to the schoolhouse at once."

"Whoa, there. Slow down. That hoss needs water and I reckon you do too. Come, bring him to the water trough. Then tell me what's the fuss." As the rider dismounted, Levi extended his hand. "I'm Levi Oakes."

"Josh Childers."

"Now, what's all the gol' darn panic?" Levi questioned.

"Well, sir, some Dakota Injuns broke into the store house near New Ulm, over in Minnesota Territory and went on a rampage slaughterin' families. Now they's dispatched embassies to the Chippeways to join them to regain their lost hunting grounds. We've got to gather everybody to stop them and keep us safe. Hurry! I've got to warn others." With that, Josh quickly remounted and urged the horse to a gallop.

Watching him go, Levi frowned. Mary ran up and linked her arm through his. "What was that all about?"

"I can't believe it. He said Indians are coming and we should git to the schoolhouse." He scowled and shook his head, "I don't see the Chippewa joining their old enemies, the Dakota. Besides, New Ulm is afar piece from here."

"The Chippewa have always been friendly here," Mary responded.

"They're good people," Levi mused, remembering his Indian nursemaid in the lumber camp. He sighed. "We'll keep a lookout for any sign of trouble, but we don't need to rush to the schoolhouse."

Mary nodded. "I'll keep the little ones close." She hollered, "Boys, come here." Brookins, Albion, and Silas ran up from Paper Jack Creek where they were catching frogs. "Brookins, Albion, you go with Pa and stay close. Silas, come with me." Mary extended her hand to four-year-old Silas. She led him to the house where she checked on baby Charles asleep in his cradle.

The older boys looked at each other and shrugged. Mary's firm tone left no room for argument. They ran after Levi headed for the horse barn. He took a bridle from the hook. "Boys, go get Duke, put on his bridle and tie him near the house."

"Pa, are we goin' to town?" Brookins inquired.

"Maybe, maybe not." Levi headed back to the house. Inside the back door, he took down the Kentucky long rifle from the rack, loaded it and returned it to the rack.

As the day wore on, wagons full of people and supplies hurried north to town. Occasionally a wagon loaded with a family and as many possessions as they could tie on headed east. Levi moseyed up the lane to talk to a family. "Where ya' headed?" he asked.

"Haven't you heard the redskins are slaughterin' settlers over in Minnesota? Why they're scalpin' women and children and burnin' everything. We're gettin' out a here before those devils' git here."

"We've got peaceful Indians here," Levi retorted.

"Don't be a fool, man. Git out while you can." The man prodded the oxen and the wagon rolled on.

That night, whenever he heard a noise, Levi rose. The dawn came and all was still quiet. It was an uneasy time. Rumors flew as settlers passed on what they heard. One story told of 150 braves in war paint on the Chippewa River north of Eau Claire. Panic subsided as no attacks came. Settlers returned to their farms, but people remained alert throughout the fall.

Paper Jack often arrived about suppertime with newspapers from Hudson and stayed the night. That gave Levi time to talk with him about the news of the Indian uprising. Jack waxed long, "Some says it's the government's fault. The Indian agent where the food was stockpiled refused to open the storehouse to the starvin' Injuns. He claimed he needed orders from Washington. The Injuns says treaties of 1858 gave them the food. I heard that the Agent tol' 'em if they're hungry let them eat grass or their own dung. What do you think of that?" Jack laughed and slapped his leg.

"I don't know. I reckon, if they had the food, they should a given it to the Indians. We've all had trouble 'cause of crop failures last year. Why, when Indians come here for flour and corn, we give 'em what we can. They repay us with bear meat and sometimes mallards and geese."

Jack shook his head and continued, "So some young braves broke into the storehouse and took food and blankets. Then they rode off, scalped a family, and set fire to the farm buildin's. Whoopee! That started it."

Mary was tending to the baby. The boys sat around the table and listened to the men talk. Levi smoked his pipe. He picked up the paper Jack had brought, studied the page, able to read only a few words. Handing the paper to Jack, he said, "What's it say?"

Jack scratched his head, "Well er...."

"Pa, I can read it," Brookins broke in. "It says soldiers from Fort Snelling called to quell Indian uprising in the Minnesota River Valley near New Ulm. The soldiers rounded up two thousand Indians and put them in the stockade at the Fort. One soldier said it was durance vile (French: confined against their will)."

"Guess that'll teach 'em a lesson," Jack beamed.

"I allow, maybe we'll be the ones learnin' a lesson," Levi replied.

"Man alive, Levi, in all my born days, I never met a man like you." Jack stood up. "Well, it's late. I'll just take my bedroll to your haymow. Thanks for the mighty fine vittles, Mrs. Oakes. They make a man feel right pert."

Mary smiled, "Oh, posh! It was just a few fixin's."

* * *

Life returned to normal, but Levi's back continued to bother. At supper he announced, "Tomorrow I'm to see Dr. Jones."

Mary frowned, "Maybe Albion should accompany you."

"Oh, I'll be fine," Levi assured her as he reached for her hand.

That evening he returned and handed the doctor's report to Mary. She took it and read:

I examined Mr. Levi Oakes. I have attended him for the preceding 5 years. I believe Levi wholly unfit for performing hard labor. At times he is troubled with spasms caused by lightning. Since that time his nervous system has been so susceptible that any loud noise such as the beating of drums, firing of cannon etc. would cause him to have spasms. He is also troubled with rheumatism so that at times he is unable to travel.

Richmond, August 22, 1862
A. Jones, M.D.

Note

1. The doctor's exam report was found among Levi's papers from his granddaughter Mildred Oakes Wilcox, daughter of Silas and Mary Amelia. Perhaps it was used for the Civil War service, but that is unknown.

15.

Elections, 1868

"Let Us Have Peace."
—Ulysses S. Grant Campaign Slogan

Indian Summer, with its riot of colors on the sugar maples, oaks, and birch, had passed. The rush of harvest was over. The root cellar was full of potatoes, carrots, rutabagas, turnips, and parsnips. Oats, rye, and wheat overflowed the granary. The house had been banked with straw and manure to keep out the cold.

November—that time of gloom before the snow—had arrived. It seemed the world was all gray. Trees, without their leaves, stood black against the dark sky. The ground was frozen as the earth slept. So, too, farmers could now rest a bit.

The evening meal had been cleared, the dishes washed and the candles lit. The family gathered around the kitchen table.

"Silas, help me with my letters," Charlie begged as he brought his slate and chalk.

"Sure," Silas moved his chair close.

"That's the way," Levi nodded his approval. "At your age is the best time to learn." He lit his pipe and watched the boys.

Brookins took out a whetstone and his pocketknife to sharpen it. Albion was whittling a willow whistle. Mary was knitting socks, the homespun wool soft in her hands.

A knock at the door startled them, and before anyone could get there, Timothy bustled in. "Uncle Timothy! Uncle Timothy!" the two younger boys jumped up to grab his legs.

"Whoa, young'uns! Let me get out of my Mackinaw." Timothy hung his coat on a peg by the door and strode to the cook stove. He rubbed his hands and held them close to warm them. He turned to look at Levi with dancing eyes, "I wondered if I might carry your ballot tomorrow when I go to vote?"

Levi leaned back in his chair shaking with laughter, "That's mighty kind of you, Mr. Oakes, but I'll carry my own."

Both men continued to shake with laughter. Brookins, Albion, Silas, and Charlie looked at each other and shrugged. Timothy pulled up a chair next to Albion, who ventured, "What's the joke?"

"Boys, your pa here was a cheat, robbing our Uncle Eben of his vote." Timothy thumped Albion on the back. "And you know every man must vote in this wonderful United States."

"Go on, with you, Tim. I was only doin' what Uncle asked," Levi countered.

"Ha! I can say he didn't see it that way," Timothy shook his head.

"So, what happened?" Brookins broke in.

"I was workin' in Uncle Eben's lumber camp, up in Aroostook, that's northern Maine. I was goin' to town and Uncle asked me to carry his ballot, seein' it was election day. So, I carried it all day," Levi chuckled.

"Tell 'em the rest of the story," Timothy urged.

"Nothin' to tell," Levi shrugged.

"Of course, there is. That night you returned the ballot to Uncle Eben, telling him: 'Here it is. I did as you asked. I carried it all day.'"

The boys jumped up, whooping, and hollering, dancing around the kitchen. "That's a good joke," Silas shouted.

"Was Uncle mad?" Albion inquired.

"Let's just say he wasn't pleased," Levi admitted.

"Come on, Levi, fess up. You looked at his ballot and didn't like who he'd voted for," Timothy laughed.

"The Republicans had a bad platform that year," Levi protested. "They shouldn't have won, but they did anyway."

"What's a platform?" Silas frowned.

"You know we have several political parties. In Maine we called 'em National Republicans but in New York they were Whigs. A platform is what they want the government to do." Levi explained.

"Is that bad?" Brookins puzzled.

"That year it was. I believe it was 1848. The Republicans were against goin' into Texas, even though Zachary Taylor won the battles in Mexico. It didn't make sense."

"So, you don't want me to carry your ballot tomorrow?" Timothy grinned.

"Naw, I can do it. Maybe you're not to be trusted," Levi winked. "I'll catch a ride with you."

"I read it to Pa, and we voted for Mr. Grant." Silas announced.

Timothy nodded, "I reckon this family is Republican still."

"Fellows at school say Grant is a drunk," Brookins interjected.

"Ah, that's a rumor. Politicians just call names," Timothy responded.

"I like that Grant doesn't call names. He's just at home receiving people," Levi added.

"Republicans say we need to keep some army in the south and the Democrats say the army should go home so there really is peace. I don't know who to believe," Brookins ventured.

"We need to keep an eye on those Southerners. If we send the army home, who knows what those rascals calling themselves Ku Klux Klan would do," Levi answered.

"I agree. The present company is grand, but I must get back before Angelina thinks me dead," Timothy smiled as he rose.

Mary looked up from her knitting, "Greet her for me."

"Sure thing." With a gust of cold air, Timothy was gone.

16.

Brookins

"Even sorrow has a silver lining."
—Rob Kozak

"Ma, I'm going east to find my pa," Brookins announced in the summer of 1869. "I've been savin' and have enough to get to Pennsylvania."

With a sad heart, Mary helped him pack. She mused, "He's an adult, let go." A few days later she hugged him goodbye.

About a month later, as Mary was kneading bread, she heard two-year-old William call out from the back step, "Brookie, Brookie." Looking out the window, she saw Brookins coming down the lane. He came in, dropped his bag, and hugged his mother. She looked at him with questioning eyes.

Brookins shook his head. "It's good to be home." He sat down at the table and munched the cookies Mary set on the table. "I got there and asked in the barbershop if anyone knew where I could find John Heacock. The barber pointed to a man across the street and said, 'You're lookin' at him.' I couldn't believe what I saw. He was wearing a silk top hat, a fancy cravat, and shoe spats, and carried a cane. That Jim Dandy was too embarrassing; I never even said howdy. The barber said he's the Methodist preacher. Now I know why you always said it was just as well he divorced you." He sat staring into space.

Mary sat down at the table. "Yes, it was best. We have a good life here. I'm sorry you were disappointed."

He stood, picked up his bag and commented, "I hear there's work in Hudson at the sawmill, so I'm gonna' mosey over there." After that Brookins spelled his name Heacox and had no time for Methodist ministers.

17.

Tragedy Strikes

"To weep is to make less the depth of grief."
—William Shakespeare, *Henry VI*

Life on the farm continued its seasonal cycles with relative calm for several years. Then the winter of 1871-72 brought tragedy. That winter many were sick with fever and the worst sore throats anyone could remember. Illness was attributed to bad air and internal imbalances; home remedies included those to draw out poisons—emetics, laxatives, enemas, plasters, and poultices. Every morning Mary opened bedroom windows to clear the bad air and she hung the blankets on the clothesline and beat them with a stick. She added camphor to a pot of simmering water on the cookstove so they could breathe the vapors. The previous summer, Mary had gathered wild horehound leaves, mint, and wild ginger in the woods and dried them. The mint and ginger leaves were used for tea. She took some dried horehound leaves and crushed them into a pan of boiling water, simmered for an hour and strained out the leaves. The liquid was boiled down until it was about half gone, stirred into honey, and bottled for cough syrup. At bedtime, each sick child gargled hot salt water and got a spoon of the horehound syrup.

Mary noticed that those that slept in the same bed with a sick child got sick faster, and baby Fred, still in his own crib, did not get sick. Mary was the last to come down with the fever just after Christmas. By mid-January, everyone seemed to have recovered except Mary, who continued to cough and tire easily. On the first of February, she suddenly was overcome with chills, fever, vomiting, and great fatigue. She did not want to eat and could not get out of bed.

Two days later, a rash broke out across her cheeks and nose. It was bright red, hot, swollen, and bumpy, like an orange peel with shiny spots.

Angelina came to peek at it. "It looks like what people call erysipelas, or St. Anthony's Fire. They say there isn't much to be done. Sometimes getting the pimples to open and drain helps. We'd better get a mustard plaster on her face," Angelina observed. She helped Levi that day. In the evening, she offered, "Why don't I take Fred home with me?"

"Oh, thank you," Levi squeezed her hand. He was so worried and having Fred cared for was such a relief.

Mary seemed to be worse each day. The boys gathered all the pillows to prop her up in bed so she could breathe. She breathed like a fish, gasping for air through her mouth. Outside it was bitterly cold, and a snowstorm blew in leaving 3 feet of snow and drifts up to 8 feet high. The boys took turns shoveling a path to the cow barn. When one was too cold, he'd come in to warm by the fire and another brother would bundle up and go shovel.

By February 8, the rash was turning black. Timothy came on snowshoes to check on them. He shook his head, "Levi, I think you should send for that new doctor in town."

"Yes, but what can he do?" Levi looked weary.

"I don't know, but maybe he has some new ideas."

"Okay. I'll send Albion with an extra pair of snowshoes for the doctor."

It was dark by the time Albion returned with Dr. Seems. The doctor examined Mary's rash shaking his head. He returned to the kitchen. He put his hand on Levi's shoulder. "She has black erysipelas. I gave her a shot of morphine to keep her more comfortable. When erysipelas turns black, mortification comes soon." It was too late for the doctor to return home, so they fixed him a place on the daybed. In the morning, he gave Mary another shot of morphine. "Try to give her some boiled milk and toast," he instructed before he left.

Mary died on February 10, 1872, at age 37 years, seven months, and seven days, leaving behind her beloved husband and six sons: Brookins (21), Albion (16), Silas (14), Charles (10), William (6), and Fred (18 months).

With shoulders slouched and head bent, Levi pulled on his boots, wrapped a muffler around his neck, pulled his beaver cap over his ears and struggled into the heavy Mackinaw. As he put on his mittens he said, "I'll go make a casket."

Silas and Albion chorused, "We'll help,"

Levi raised his hand to stop them. "No, I'll do this. Just leave me alone," he growled. He stomped off to the barn to be alone with his grief. When the casket was finished, he called the boys to help carry it to the parlor.

Angelina spread a quilt in the box. Levi went up to the bedroom and gently picked up Mary's body. He carried her to the casket and laid her down. The storm continued, hence no funeral. Timothy and his family tromped through the snow for a service with Bible readings, singing, and prayers.

Angelina announced, "Dinner is ready." She had brought food for dinner and enough to last another day.

After dinner, Levi carefully wrapped the quilt around Mary and placed the top on the casket and nailed it shut. The men carried it to the hay barn because there was no way to get a wagon and team of horses through the deep snow to the cemetery. Usually when someone died in the winter, the casket was placed in the tool shed at the cemetery until spring when the ground thawed so a grave could be dug.

* * *

The next couple of months were a blur for Levi. He didn't laugh and tease in the old way. Somehow, he survived. He and the boys learned to cook and keep little Fred always with them. In late March, the snow was mostly gone. As the sun began to thaw the ground, they could dig a grave. It was slow since the frost line was about 5 feet underground. They finished digging and called on the Methodist minister at the new church on 2nd Street. A graveside service was arranged for the following week.

All the neighbors came. The pastor spoke and they sang. The men took turns shoveling dirt over the coffin. After the last shovel of dirt was replaced, Levi took off his hat and bowed his head.

Brookins, now married, made the trip from Hudson with his wife, Matilda, daughter, Elva, and son, George. After the funeral, Brookins didn't come to the farm again. Hudson was 15 miles away and a long trip by horse and buggy. Little did anyone know that it would be 50 years before the family reconnected with Brookins' family.

Note

1. Erysipelas is a strep infection of the skin, often on the face or hands and toes. It is often secondary to injury. In Mary's case, the adenoids filling her nostrils harbored strep bacteria. When the rash turns black, gangrene has set in and is usually fatal.

18.

Not in This House

The first hard frost turned the red maples along the driveway to brilliant crimson. The fallen leaves were blown into piles. Fred exuberantly kicked through the piles as he hurried home from school. Down the hill, he saw Pa tending a fire under the huge cast iron kettle hanging from the iron tripod. He ran by William shouting, "Race ya."

William turned on the speed, but Fred touched the back step barely ahead of Will. "Ha ha I beat," Fred crowed.

"Only because you cheated, little brother," Will retorted, as he playfully punched him on the shoulder.

They dropped their lunch buckets on the step and hurried on to see what Pa was doing. He was rendering the tallow from the ewe he had butchered yesterday. A table was set nearby with all the supplies for candle making. Pa looked up and grinned, "Hello, boys. You're just in time to help. Will, take the wooden paddle and skim off the chitlins. Fred, hold the pan for Will."

Will stirred the pot and skimmed off the chitlins, dumping them into the pan Fred held. When they finished, they set the pan to cool. They watched Pa carefully thread the wick cords through the mold. Pa had made the tin mold with divisions for six candles at a time.

"Pa, why don't we have modern kerosene lamps?" Fred inquired.

"NO! I will never have those goldarn death traps in my house," Pa roared. He shook, leaned against the table, and stared across the field toward Paper Jack Creek.

"Pa, what's wrong?" Will said with alarm. Frightened, both boys stepped over, one on each side of him. They each put an arm around him.

It seemed forever before Pa sighed, "Sorry, I was remembering that awful night."

William asked innocently, "Ya mean when you were struck by lightning?"

"Yah, for sure. When the lightning struck, the kerosene lantern exploded, and the tent burned in a flash. I never want a fire like that, so we're not having those dangerous abominations."

"But, Pa, how did you get out of that fire?" Fred pestered.

"I don't know. They tell me a search party found the three of us and I was the only one alive laying in a pool of water. I woke up back at camp. When I finally could get up, I had this gimpy limb." He slapped his leg in disgust. "No siree, there will never be kerosene lamps in this house. Tallow candles work just fine and won't explode. Yah, I know the neighbors think I'm touched, but that's okay by me."

"Folks also say you have a weird farm with the buildings so far apart. They say you must like to have your boys shovel snow to get to the cow barn and stable," Will laughed.

"Well, boys, you can bet the whole farm won't burn if a fire gets one building," Pa bragged. "See, the house is close to the road, up the hill, where I can see down to the creek and all the buildings." He swept his arm from left to right, pointing to the buildings.

Fred and Will turned and looked where Pa was pointing. The cow barn, near the creek was about a couple hundred feet below the house, and the horse stable was more than the length of a football field away along the creek. It was built into the hillside with 18-square-inch limestone blocks. Only the roof and door were wood.

Levi's house south side facing Paper Jack Creek. Open well in front has very long handle for easier pumping.

Remains of Levi's horse barn built 1856 with sandstone quarried on his property. Oakes Ruins Project started Oct. 2023 to restore the barn.

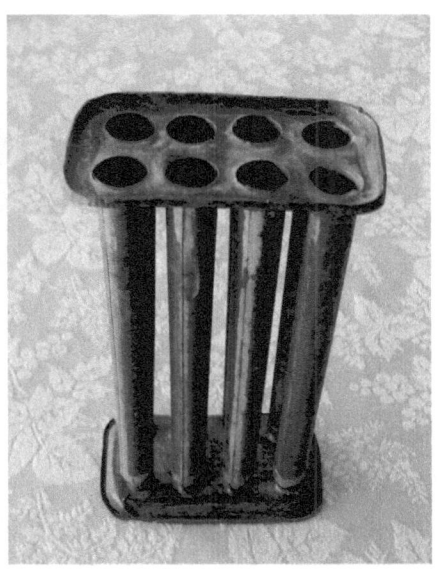

Tin candle mold made by Levi J. Oakes, ca. 1857.

Candle made with Levi's mold by great granddaughter Launa
Oakes Morasch, 2000.

Levi Jefferson Oakes

Mary Potter Heacock Oakes (Levi's first wife)

Mary Markley Morgan Oakes (Levi's second wife)

Wedding photo, Feb. 13, 1896, Fred Moses Oakes

Wedding photo, Hannah Andersen Oakes

At Oakes Grove farm on the north side of Paper Jack Creek,1904.
L to R: Fred M. Hannah, Ardis, Esther, Florence, and Fred Arthur

Hannah's Iver Johnson .32 revolver, passed on to her son Hollis and then to his son Bruce. It is 5 inches overall with a 2-inch barrel.

Levi Jefferson Oakes, March 4, 1907. He died March 8, 1907.

George Oakes, son of Timothy and Angelina, nephew of Levi

Modern Headstone on Oakes Family Plot erected by Esther
Oakes Carson and Fred A. Oakes, New Richmond City Cemetery.
Levi's birthdate corrected by Fred A. Oakes.

Daughters of Fred M. & Hannah Oakes, 1909.
L to R, Back row: Esther, 12; Florence, 9; Ardis, 7.
L to R, Front row: Elsinore, 6; Ruth, 4; Viola, 2.

First Reunion of Oakes and Heacox families, June 4, 1922, at
Fred M. and Hannah Oakes farm near Balsam Lake, Georgetown
Township, Polk County, Wisconsin.

Fiftieth wedding anniversary of Fred M. and Hannah Oakes, Feb. 13, 1946, with children and grandchildren. L to R: Hollis, Kay (author), Florence, Hannah, Ruth, Bruce, Viola, Fred M., Fred A.

Sons of Levi and Mary Potter Oakes, 1923. L to R, Top row: William, Charles, Fred M., Silas. L to R, Bottom row: Hannah, wife of Fred M.; Annie, wife of Charles; Tena, second wife of Silas.

19.

Changes

"Change, like healing, takes time."
—Veronica Roth

Spring 1873

The demands of plowing, planting, haying, and harvesting, in addition to cooking, cleaning, and washing clothes kept Levi too busy to think of his loss. Often Timothy and Angelina invited Levi and his sons for supper. Their daughters, Della and Ida, liked to play with little Fred.

Timothy ambled over to Levi's house one warm spring day. "Hello!" he laughed. "I heard that's the new city slicker way to say 'Howdy.'"

Both snickered.

Levi shook his head and swatted a large mosquito on his hand, "Dang, these gol' darn nippers are early this year."

"Yep. We might have to beat a hasty retreat to the house. You know, Dr. Bell has been wanting to buy my place. I found a fine piece of land up by Clear Lake, so I took the doctor up on his offer. We'll be skedaddling soon."

"Sure hate to see you go, but I know you've been itchin' to try a new place," Levi replied. "Clear Lake must be at least 20 miles up there, isn't it?"

"I reckon," Timothy agreed.

After Timothy and his family moved, it seemed too quiet. "Nine young'uns underfoot make a lot more racket," Levi observed. "Guess I have plenty of ankle biters of my own."

Fall 1875

Albion (now 19 years old) came tearing into the barn, shouting, "Pa, where are you?"

Levi looked down from the hay mow where he was pitching hay down onto the wagon. "Right here, son. What's the big hurry?"

"There's the handsomest little Morgan hoss for sale at the auction house. I fancy that one. If you'd help me buy her, I'll work it off or go loggin' this winter. Please Pa, please Pa."

"Hold yur hosses. Help me get this hay over to the cows and then we'll go have a peek."

Albion was thrilled, "You won't be sorry, Pa. She's a beaut, and I heard those Morgan's are really strong."

That evening, they returned with the beautiful filly. She was a little nervous, so Albion walked her around the farm, so she'd get familiar with it. He put her in a stall in the horse barn for the night. In the morning, he hurried out to see her. She shied and kicked, catching Albion across his right limb. He could feel blood running down his leg. "Oh, crap," he muttered under his breath. He didn't want Pa to find out. He took a rag and wrapped the leg. Later he would get a dish towel and go wash it by the well when no one was looking. His attempt to hide the wound didn't work. A few days later he had a fever, and the leg was so painful he couldn't step on it.

"Let's see what's wrong with that limb," Levi demanded. He looked at the inflamed, infected leg, "How in thunder did this happen?"

"The filly kicked me," Albion whispered.

The poultices didn't draw out the poison and a couple of days later Albion died. With great sadness, Levi dug the third grave in the family plot.

Fall 1876

"Pa, I can't get into these pants anymore," 14-year-old Charlie exclaimed, "And look at my shirt." He held out his arms to show Levi that the long sleeves came just past his elbows.

"Posh," Levi laughed, "you all need clothes. I'll ask around about a seamstress."

Seamstresses of the time were often spinsters who moved with their treadle sewing machines from farm-to-farm sewing clothes for each family. When Levi was next in town, he asked at the general store, "Do you know a seamstress I could hire to make clothes for my boys?"

"I heard Widow Morgan was sewing over at the Bailey place," the proprietress replied. "Thanks, I'll go by their place."

When Levi arrived at home, he announced, "You boys'll get new clothes soon. Mrs. Morgan is coming next week."

On Friday morning, Mr. Bailey came in his horse-drawn wagon bearing Mrs. Morgan and her two children: Mary Amelia (12) and Hall (10). Tied in the back of the wagon was her Singer treadle sewing machine, plus two small trunks. Mary Markley Morgan was a short, stout woman with fair-skin and deep-set blue eyes. Her blond hair was parted in the middle with waves along her face and pulled back into a bun. Her nose was broad above thin unsmiling lips.

Levi and the boys ran out to greet them. Mr. Bailey jumped down and tied the horse to the hitching post. Levi stepped forward saying "Welcome," as he helped Mrs. Morgan down. Mary Amelia and Hall jumped over the side of the wagon and stood staring at the boys. "Boys, meet Mrs. Morgan, Mary Amelia, and Hall." He turned and pointed. "These are my boys, Silas, Charles, William, and Fred."

"Pa, you didn't tell us there were goin' be children to play with," 10-year-old William clamored.

Levi winked. "I thought I'd surprise you."

Mary Morgan quickly settled in, took the boys' measurements, and sewed. A take-charge kind of person, she soon managed the whole household. The boys were awed and amused by her crusty demeanor. She smoked a pipe, which seemed to always be in her mouth. She would hold it with her teeth out one side of her mouth while she talked and worked. Sometimes ashes fell into the food she was preparing. She'd set aside the pipe to scoop up the ashes, exclaiming, "Oh, shit." The boys giggled. She took fresh hot bread and tea out to the field where Levi was plowing. "Thank you, Mary, your bread is so delicious," Levi smacked his lips.

"You're welcome." Mary Morgan leaned against the plow, "Ain't days like this worth a heap o' Sundays?"

"Sure are," Levi responded as he moved closer. "I've been ponderin'—we get along so swell, maybe we should get hitched."

"Far be it from me to object," Mary's eyes twinkled as she reached out and squeezed his hand. "We could drive over to Hudson and get married. There's a Justice of the Peace there." They were married October 23, 1876, (three days after she moved in) by John Duffy, Justice of the Peace. Witnesses were Frank Chapman and Silas Oakes. Mary Morgan was 59 years old; Levi was 51.

Levi joked with her, "I have to do what you say because you're older than me."

Levi looked around the dinner table after the wedding. "Six—the magic number. We always seem to have six young'uns at this table." Silas (18), Charlie (14), William (10), Fred (6), Mary Amelia (14), and Hall (12).

Mary Morgan loved her new family. "You boys treat me better than my own children."

* * *

Mary Morgan called her daughter, Mary Amelia, my delicate one. She was the same age as Charlie. He soon learned he could tease her and get a great reaction. One day he was skipping rocks across Paper Jack Creek when Mary Amelia came walking along and stopped to watch him.

"I can do that," she announced.

"Bet ya can't," Charlie grinned mischievously. As they skipped rocks, he asked, "Is it true that your pa was killed in a drunken brawl in Hudson?"

Her eyes snapped, "Charlie Oakes, it's not your funeral so bug off."

"I just wondered if it's true he had a brick in his hat," Charlie shrugged.

"You're mean, Charlie Oakes!" Mary Amelia turned and ran toward the woods. Her head down, she ran headlong into Silas. He caught her by the hands. "Hey, little one, what's wrong?"

Mary Amelia just sobbed. "Come on, out with it," Silas said softly. Mary Amelia only sobbed more. "Come, sit here in the shade and tell me what's wrong."

"Charlie is so mean."

"What did he do?" Silas demanded.

Suddenly Mary Amelia was angry, "I hate him. Why don't people leave me alone?"

"What happened? It's okay to tell me. I'll tan his hide if he hurt you."

Mary Amelia laughed in spite of herself. The thought of Silas licking Charlie was funny.

"No, he didn't hurt me. He asked if it was true about my pa."

"What's true?" Silas looked troubled.

"My pa died after a fight. I guess they were corned (drunk). I don't know. It happened when I was little. My sister told me because Ma won't talk about it."

"I'm sorry," Silas hung his head not knowing what else to say. Then he looked up, "I didn't know you had a sister."

"I have two older sisters. They're both working as hired girls on farms near Hudson." Mary Amelia was happy to change the subject.

"Well, if Charlie bothers you again, just tell me," Silas smiled at her as they walked toward the house.

"Thank you," Mary Amelia smiled back.

Right now, Silas thought of her only as a child that needed comforting. Little did he imagine how his feelings would change.

* * *

Before returning to River Falls, Levi questioned Silas, "How is it goin' with the family in River Falls?"

In exchange for room and board, Silas chopped wood, kept the wood boxes full and did any job they asked. "It's workin' out."

"Are you behavin' yourself?"

"Sure, Pa."

August 1878

It was a hot August day as Levi and the boys finished harvest. It was almost time for Charlie to head back to River Falls to high school. Silas had finished high school the year before and had worked during the winter as a carpenter's assistant. Now he had other ideas. "Pa, what do you think of me going back to River Falls Normal School? I've been thinking that teaching school might be good."

Levi stared at Silas. "Well, I'll be a monkey's uncle! That's what you want?"

"Yep, that's about the size of it," Silas grinned.

Two weeks later, Levi took the horse and buggy with Silas and Charlie to River Falls. As they said goodbye, Silas noticed how pretty Mary Amelia was. She blushed when he gave her a peck on the cheek. Silas noticed that his hands were sweaty and his heart racing. "Stop it," he told himself, "She has a beau."

Mary Amelia was 16. Since she finished eighth grade, she stayed home. The Grimes boy from down the road was a regular caller at the Oakes farm.

Levi remarked to Mary Morgan, "I think that boy has designs on your delicate one."

"Humph! Maybe she'll see the elephant."

1880

"Ma, me and George are aimin' to get hitched," Mary Amelia announced.

"Horse feathers! You're not ready." Mary Morgan removed the pipe from her mouth and shook it at her delicate one.

"I'm 18."

The wedding was held in June. Silas and Charlie had returned from school, both graduated. Silas was ready to start teaching and Charlie had finished high school. Silas watched Mary Amelia closely, "I hope she's happy," he thought.

1882

When the school term was finished in May, Silas resigned. Teaching wasn't for him. He returned to the farm to help with the spring planting. He was surprised to find Mary Amelia at home without one-year old baby George. "What a surprise. Are you visiting? Where's little George?"

"No, I left. It didn't work out," Mary Amelia replied. "That lout insisted on keeping his son. What are you doing? Ma said you resigned your teaching post."

"Yep, it wasn't all it was cracked up to be."

"What are ya goin' do?"

"I think I'll head up to Superior. The railroad is laying tracks there and the pay is good."

Silas went in search of Charlie. "Hey, why don't you come with me to Superior?"

"That sounds great," Charlie responded. "Remember how much fun we had when the train reached New Richmond? Everyone turned out to help lay tracks. All the townsmen and farmers worked hard while the women served up lots of grub. We kids had fun playing."

"Yah, I remember. That's why I thought it would be good to go to Superior." The brothers left to work on laying rails. Silas wrote to Mary Amelia and in the fall asked her to marry him. She quickly consented. With the rail line completed, the brothers returned home. Silas and Mary Amelia married in Oakes Grove and lived nearby for several years.

Mary Morgan observed, "Sure is quiet in the house these days." She sighed, "I wish I knew where Hall is. That boy always had a hankerin' to wander."

"It surely is different," Levi patted her shoulder. "Maybe Hall will write or come home after he's seen the world."

"It would be nice to have a crystal ball to see what comes next," Mary Morgan said, as she puffed on her pipe.

20.

Silas and Mary Amelia

"Love me when I least deserve it because that's when I really need it."

—Swedish proverb

After the wedding, Silas and Mary Amelia rented a farm near Oakes Grove. Silas cherished his delicate wife, feeling so needed. Mary Amelia soon announced, "There's a wee one in the oven."

"Are you sure?"

"Of course, silly."

Taking her face in both hands, Silas kissed her passionately on the mouth. He released her and laughed, "I'm going to be a father!" He took her in his arms and danced her around the kitchen and pulled her outside and shouted to the universe, "I'm going to be a father!"

Mary Amelia giggled as she nestled against him, "I'm so happy." But the pregnancy took its toll. Some days she couldn't get out of bed. Other days she sat and cried, twisting a handkerchief around her fingers, and dabbing her eyes.

Perplexed, Silas sought advice from his pa and stepma. He arrived at Oakes Grove shortly after breakfast.

"Mornin', son," Levi boomed.

"Mornin', Pa."

Ma stepped out of the house, "Land sakes, you're out 'n about early. How about a cup o' coffee?"

"That would be swell."

Ma bustled about setting out coffee cups and a plate of fresh rolls and butter.

Silas sighed, "Ma, I don't know what to do about Mary Amelia. I thought she was happy about the baby, but she cries all the time."

Ma reached over and patted his hand, "I know, women with child can be pretty weepy. It's alright. She'll get over it."

"I don't know, she can't seem to get up to do anything some days."

"Oh, my delicate one takes everything so hard," Ma mused. "I'll come by this afternoon.

Levi chuckled, "Ma's right. I think havin' a baby is sometimes harder on the father. Why, when the cryin's over, she'll be bitin' your head off. Then when that squallin' baby pops out, she'll soon be sweet as honey."

"I hope you're right," Silas sighed again, frowning, his shoulders slumped.

"Course I am. Come on, let's go check on the corn field and watch it grow," Levi winked as he rose from the table. "Thanks for the coffee, Ma."

"You're welcome." She turned to Silas, "I'll be by after dinner."

"Thanks, Ma. You always seem to calm her down."

At noon, Levi and the sons still living at home—Charlie, William, and Fred—came in from the field, washed at the basin by the backdoor and sat down at the kitchen table. Everyone bowed their heads as Levi prayed, "Dear Lord, bless our souls and bodies as we partake of these fine vittles from your bounty. In Jesus' name, Amen."

Everyone dug into the steaming bowls of baked beans, creamed peas, and new potatoes fresh from the garden and rye bread hot from the oven. Comfortably, they ate in silence, each engrossed in filling their growling stomachs. Charlie reached across William's plate to grab the bread, "Excuse my boarding-house-reach." William pretended to stab Charlie with his fork. They both laughed.

Ma served up a delicious rhubarb custard pie. As they finished, she instructed Fred, "Bring the small cart up to the house. I'm going to walk over to Silas and Mary Amelia's with some things."

Ma loaded up bread in a basket, a pot of beans, the leftover peas and potatoes, and a pie. Pulling the cart, she walked briskly down the road. Knocking on the back door, Ma waited. There was no answer. Opening the door, she called, "Mary Amelia?"

"Come in," came the weak response from the parlor.

Stepping into the kitchen, she surveyed the room. Breakfast dishes were still on the table and the sink was piled high with dirty dishes. "I brought some things for your supper. I'll just put them away." In the summer, food was stored in the root cellar a few paces from the house.

Opening the heavy door, the rush of cold air was most welcome on this warm August day. The cold air and earthy smell were somehow comforting as Ma set the food on a shelf. Back inside the house, Ma found Mary Amelia sitting in the parlor staring into space. "Oh, my dear, what's wrong?"

"Mama, I don't know. I just can't stop crying," Mary Amelia sobbed.

Ma sat down on the settee next to her daughter, "There, there, it's okay. Of course, carrying a baby changes you. This cryin' will soon end. Pull yourself together. Come, let's go make a spot o'tea." She gently nudged Mary Amelia to rise and guided her to the kitchen table.

The fire was out in the cook stove. Ma expertly crumpled a newspaper in the firebox and laid kindling over it. The match struck and the flames flared. Ma watched it closely, adding more small oak firewood until there was a nice bed of red-hot coals and larger pieces added. Soon the kettle boiled; Ma filled the teapot and set it on the table to steep while she cleared the dirty dishes.

"I always found it is best to just do what ya gotta do," Ma smiled. "Then when the jobs are done, you can pour a cup o' tea and sit a spell, thankin' the Almighty for your blessings—just like we're doin."

"Mama, maybe I'm not cut out to be a wife and mother."

"Oh, posh! You'll be fine."

"But I've already messed up my first marriage and lost little George."

"That Mr. Grimes messed up your marriage and was so pig-headed about keeping his son. I was against that man from the first time I laid eyes on him. The past is past. Put it behind you. Silas is a good man, and he loves you. You'll do just ducky."

January 18, 1883

A raw wind was blowing when Mary Amelia awakened. "What is this pain?" she thought sleepily. Fully awake, she sat up with the next contraction. "Silas, Silas, wake up. Go get Ma; it's time."

Silas rolled over as she pounded on him. He caught her hands, "Whoa, baby. I'm going."

"Hurry," she gasped with the next contraction. Lying back on the bed, it seemed Silas should be gone; however, she heard him stoking the fire. "Go get Ma. I need her now," she screamed.

An eternity passed before Silas returned with Ma and a neighbor lady. Ma took charge, "Get more pots of water on the stove. Bring the warm one and all the cloth we prepared to the bedroom." Just then they heard a scream from the bedroom. "That war whoop must mean it's almost here." She ran to the bedroom. Mary Amelia lay panting on the bed. Ma saw that Silas had already installed the rope at on headboard for Mary Amelia to hold on to and stirrups at the footboard for her feet.

"Get more pillows." Propping her up, Ma instructed, "Hang on to the rope and press your feet against the footboard. When the next contraction comes, bite down on this wet washcloth and push hard."

A few hard pushes with accompanying war whoops, and out popped a red wrinkled girl. Ma held her up and smacked her on the butt. The baby gave a startled cry. Ma swaddled her and laid her on Mary Amelia's chest, while she tied and cut the umbilical cord. Exhausted, Mary Amelia whispered, "Isn't she beautiful?"

Silas approached and kissed her, "Yes, and so are you." He, too, was exhausted. He thought, "It's like a cow having a calf."

Mary Amelia ran her finger across the baby's face, tracing her eyes, nose, and mouth. "Mildred Mae is a fine name for her."

21.

Silas and Mary Amelia
and Charlie and Anna

"Take my hand and we can get through this together."
—Unknown

Silas loved Mary Amelia deeply but keeping up with the farm and soothing his wife kept him exhausted. In the summer of 1883, as Mildred learned to crawl, Mary Amelia took delight in her bundle of joy and came out of her melancholia. She was delighted to be with child again, singing as she played with Mildred, cleaned the house and cooked. In August she felt the baby move. Scooping up Mildred, she hurried to the barn, "Sile, the baby is moving." Silas was sharpening an axe on the grinding wheel. Smiling, he quietly came to her side and put his arm around her.

"Here, feel here," Mary Amelia guided his hand to her abdomen. What a thrill.

A few weeks later, as Mary Amelia was putting Mildred down for a nap, she suddenly doubled over in pain. "No, it can't be. Maybe if I lie down it will stop." Moving quickly from the crib to her bed, she sat down, hurriedly unlaced her boots, slipped them off, and lay on the bed with her feet up on the footboard. "I best get Sile." But there was no time—the miscarriage came with a rush. Mary Amelia slipped back into melancholia. Ma came to help. Some days she took Mildred home with her, "Mildred and me are goin' have fun. Now you rest, Mary Amelia."

By Christmas, Mary Amelia seemed better. Everyone enjoyed Mildred as she toddled around. Levi and Mary doted on their first grandchild.

1884

After spring planting was done and before summer field-work started, there was a breather for social gatherings. Young people gathered for picnics, often drawn to Oakes Grove. There Charlie met Anna Ingebrigtsen and was immediately smitten. Silas teased his brother, "Is it her good Norwegian cookin'?"

"Oh, yah, fur sure, ya betcha," Charlie imitated Anna's Norwegian accent. A wave of Norwegian immigrants in the area brought new customs and language, which was fodder for teasing from the old timers. Anna, although born in Wisconsin, spoke Norwegian at home. Her English had the lilt of Norway.

On Sundays, Charlie and Anna often came to visit Silas, Mary Amelia, and Mildred.

Often, they brought a picnic lunch, spread blankets on the clover field by the house, and relaxed. If the mosquitoes were too bad, they retreated to the new screen porch, which Charlie admired, "This new-fangled wire mesh is mighty fine."

"They say it keeps malaria away. I thought I would give it a try," Silas retorted.

The delicate one sometimes remained in bed with the shades drawn. Anna, with her easy smile and twinkling blue eyes, tried to coax her outside, "Mary Amelia, 'tis a right beautiful day and ve do vant you to yoin us. Fresh air vill do you goot." Sometimes it worked.

September was Mary Amelia's favorite month. A hard frost had killed the mosquitoes and flies and turned the maples deep crimson. The air was crystal clear with the sultry humidity of summer gone. Invigorated, Mary Amelia harvested her tomatoes and canned them. As usual on Sunday, Charlie and Anna came for dinner. They were both giggling. "Alright, spill the beans," Mary Amelia laughed.

The couple giggled again. "Well, I asked Ellef for his daughter's hand," Charlie blushed.

"Ve vill be married on the 27th of November," Anna added.

"You ole sly one," Silas slapped Charlie on the back. "So, you will launch on the sea of matrimony."

"That's wonderful. We were beginin' to wonder when you'd tie the knot," Mary Amelia teased.

"Vell, everyone gathers for this American Thanksgiving, so it seems like a goot time," Anna replied.

Thanksgiving Day dawned clear and cold with only a dusting of snow—a great day for a wedding. Family and friends arrived at Ingebrigtsen's farm in buggies or wagons not needing sleighs yet. The Lutheran preacher and his wife came along. He performed the ceremony just before dinner.

What a feast it was. All the women had outdone themselves, bringing roasted chicken, pork roasts, potatoes, carrots, and pies—apple, mincemeat, walnut. The

Norwegian women brought typical Norwegian specialties: rodkal (red cabbage cooked with apples, honey, and a little vinegar), plus fancy cookies and pastries—krumkakes, rosettes, marzipan tarts, and pebersnabber.

It was evident that Mary Amelia was again with child, so everyone took care not to upset the apple cart.

* * *

Jennie Belle made her entrance, April 23, 1885, without fanfare. This pregnancy had gone well. "Two daughters! I like that," Mary Amelia cooed.

"Well, I guess I'll have to teach them to be farm hands," Silas beamed.

"Not so fast, Sile. They'll need to learn women's work." Their happy time was short-lived as Mary Amelia had another miscarriage the next year, sending her back into melancholia. She was just returning to her sweet self when she told Silas she was again with child. He sat down, propped his elbows on his knees and held his head in his large, callused hands. Mary Amelia was right pert, "This time will be fine; I just feel it in my bones." She sat on the floor beside him and leaned her head on his lap.

A raw north wind was blowing the morning of October 6, 1887, when Silas went to fetch Ma. "It's time," was all he said. Ma hurriedly took her coat from the hook and returned to deliver a boy.

"Is he alright, Ma?" Mary Amelia propped herself up to look. "Sure is."

"A boy!" Silas was incredulous. "Let's name him Frank. That's a nice strong name." "Yes," Mary Amelia agreed. "And Morgan as his middle name for my father."

"Of course. Frank Morgan Oakes. That has a nice sound."

* * *

With each pregnancy Mary Amelia ate more and more. When Frank was almost a year old, she had another miscarriage and her first conniption fit. Frightened, Silas put the children in the wagon, hitched the horses and drove to Oakes Grove. "Ma, she just lost the baby and she's havin' a fit. Can you take the young'uns? Send Fred for the doctor. I've got to get back."

"Lawd almighty, I was afeared of this. Talk real gentle like and soft to her."

Silas nodded as he handed Frank to Ma and set Jennie Belle on the ground, while Mildred scrambled down by herself, being a big girl of five. He jumped back on the wagon seat, clucked to the horses, and then cracked the whip to set them off at a gallop.

Mary Amelia seemed to be sleeping as he tiptoed to the bedroom door. He returned to the kitchen, collapsing in a chair to wait for the doctor.

A horse whinny startled him. "Must be Doc." As he opened the kitchen door, Doc was just tying his horse to the hitching post. "Thanks for coming so quick."

"I was just headin' out this way when Fred caught me. What seems to be the problem?"

"Mary Amelia lost the baby this morning and has been screamin' enough to scare the devil. Right now, she seems to be sleeping."

"Let's see how she is."

Silas waited in the kitchen, watching the clock. It seemed forever before Doc came out and sat down. "I think she is settled now." He set a bottle of pills on the table. "I got her to take one of these. You can give her one in the morning and evening. It will calm her." He paused and studied Silas. "Silas, a big fleshy woman like she is and her delicate nature, shouldn't have any more children."

They sat in silence while this news sank in. Silas only nodded. "Maybe I will need to sleep in the spare room," he thought.

Doc stood, "I must be gettin' back. Send for me if she is worse."

"Thanks a million." Silas took out his wallet, removed a $5 greenback, and handed it to Doc.

22.

The Grass Is Always Greener

"The grass isn't always greener on the other side."
—Nick Foles

"I hear there's a heap o' work up in Superior. Folks built on swampy land and their houses are sinking. They need to drive pilings or move the houses," Charlie commented. "Are you interested in going?"

Silas nodded, "We could do that. I've been thinkin' maybe a change of scene might be good for Mary Amelia, too."

"Could be," Charlie responded.

All winter they talked about the opportunities in Superior. Anna and Mary Amelia were excited too. By Spring 1889, it was settled, and both families moved. They found adjacent houses just south of Lake Superior on West 7th Street.

The novelty of living in a town kept Mary Amelia happy for a while; however, Silas was now gone all day, busy building up a contracting business. She couldn't walk to the field to get him when she couldn't cope. Exhausted by the work of running a household and caring for three children, she was often short-tempered.

Even though Silas hired four men to help him and Charlie, by night he was dog-tired. He paused at the back door, took a deep breath, and listened. No yelling or screaming tonight.

Slowly he opened the door and stepped into the kitchen. Mildred, now nine, turned from stoking the cookstove, "Evenin', Pa."

Silas smiled, "How's my girl?" His eyes surveyed the kitchen: Seven-year-old Jennie Bell was on a stool by the sink peeling potatoes. Frank, at five years old, was too interested in spinning his top around the floor. "Where's your Ma?"

"In bed," Mildred offered as she ducked her head and averted her eyes.

"Bad day?"

"You might say." Mildred sniffled and continued, "She says we're no good and don't help. But Pa, we made the beds, scrubbed the floor, and carried the wash out to the line."

Jennie Bell just stood with tears rolling down her face.

"You are good girls and do much work." Silas scooped up Jennie Bell and patted her back as she snuggled with her head on his shoulder. "Come let's get these potatoes cooked. We'll add some salt pork, fry some eggs, and have a fine supper."

Soon supper was on the table. They ate in silence. Silas dished up a plate for Mary Amelia. "I'll take this up to Ma while you do dishes." Cautiously opening the bedroom door, Silas peered in. Mary Amelia seemed asleep. He approached the bed on tiptoe, setting the plate on the bed stand. He whispered, "Mary Amelia, are you awake?"

Startled, she sat bolt upright with a scream. "Shhh, shhh, it's just me." Her eyes were wild with no recognition of him.

"Shh, shh, you're fine. I brought you some supper. Come, try some. You must be hungry." He took some potato on the fork and held it to her mouth.

Mary Amelia sniffed and opened her mouth. Obediently she ate the proffered food.

"There, that's better. You'll feel better when you've eaten. See, the girls cooked potatoes with salt pork and fried eggs."

At the mention of the girls, Mary Amelia bristled, "Those no-good rug rats cause nothin' but trouble and aren't any help at all. And you are gone all the time. Fine state of affairs, Mr. Oakes."

Silas bit his tongue. No use fanning the fire. "You just rest. I'll see the little ones to bed." He rose and took the plate back to the kitchen.

Later Silas slumped in a chair, his elbows propped on the kitchen table, holding his head in his hands. "What am I to do?"

Someone knocked at the door. "Come in," Silas called.

Anna, his very pregnant sister-in-law, waddled in from next door. She paused, listened, and whispered, "Is she asleep?"

Silas nodded.

"Vell, it's been a hard day, I tell you. I try to get over here, but with four young'uns and another in the oven, it ain't easy."

"I know. It's mighty kind of you."

"I found a hired girl for you. Lord knows you need one. The Johnsons down the road have a daughter looking for vork, ya know."

Silas shook his head, "T'would be fine, but she'd probably not stay when Mary Amelia gets the melancholia."

"Yah, I took the liberty to talk to Christina after church on Sunday. She'll do it. I can tell her to come around on Saturday. That is, if you want."

"No harm in talkin'."

"Goot. It's settled then. Goot nat."

All week Silas talked to Mary Amelia about how they needed a hired girl to help with the cooking, cleaning, and care of the young'uns. Mary Amelia listened but said little until Friday.

"What if I don't like her?" she demanded.

"I suppose I'll look for another girl. Please give it a try."

Christina arrived at the appointed hour bringing sweets for the children.

"Oh, thank you Christina," Mildred beamed.

"Oh, everyone calls me Tena, so you may, too."

Mary Amelia eyed Tena suspiciously. "I'm very particular about my house. Do you know how to clean the cook stove and polish it with stove black?"

"Of course, Mam. I do it every week at home."

"Can you handle these three rug rats?"

"Yah, I do love children." After a few more questions, Mary Amelia caught Silas' eye and nodded.

Silas rose from his chair, "We'd be obliged to have you. You may have the spare room for your own and come as soon as you like."

"Thank you. I'll come with my valise after church tomorrow."

After Tena left, Silas bounced up, "Come, let's prepare the spare room." The children scurried to help while Mary Amelia sat and stared out the window. "Come, son, we'll get the old commode from the shed so Tena may have her morning toilette in private."

Mildred and Jennie Bell got fresh linens and a wool quilt from the cedar chest and made up the bed. Mildred turned to Jennie Bell, "That looks nice. Now we need a basin, water pitcher, and soap for the commode. Oh, and an oil lamp."

Sunday morning everyone was in high spirits in anticipation of Tena's arrival. Even Mary Amelia was smiling as she stoked the fire in the cook stove and popped the roaster filled with chicken, onions, and potatoes into the oven. "Soon there will be help with all these chores," she giggled.

Dressed in their Sunday best, they walked to the Presbyterian Church. Frank ran ahead.

Silas called, "Frank, wait for us." Frank ran back, but soon sped off again. Seated in church, the children fidgeted and watched the wall clock, anxious to be home for Tena's arrival.

Mary Amelia seemed in high spirits, greeting friends. She walked fast on the way home, "Hurry, we must have dinner ready when Tena arrives."

23.

The Delicate One

"The 'rest' cure: rest, a fattening diet, and electricity."
—Anne Stiles

"Get away! Don't touch me!" Mary Amelia screeched, breathlessly.

"There, there, I won't hurt you. You'll feel better after a cup of tea and a rest," Silas crooned. He approached her slowly, talking softly as he would to a frightened horse. "My dear, Dr. Smith says the doctors and nurses at the hospital will help you."

"I don't need help; everyone is just against me."

"I know you want to be a good mother. You'll have fresh air and a rest away from all the work and worries. You'll come home refreshed."

"Sile, I'm scared." Mary Amelia's face was white, and her eyes were bulging.

"It will be fine. Come, it's time to go." He reached out and took her hand. The outburst over, she stood and leaned against him.

October 27, 1894, was etched in his mind. That day he had his dear wife committed to the insane asylum. He shuddered, shook himself, and sighed. "I had to do this," he told himself. "There was no way we could manage her at home. She was hitting the children and Tena; her screams upsetting the whole neighborhood."

For three weeks there was calm in the household. Tena managed the house and children with quiet efficiency while Silas turned his attention to his business. The autumn was unusually warm, and he could keep a crew working moving houses that had been built on swampy land to higher ground. Just as they were sitting down to supper, a knock at the door brought a messenger.

"I have a message for Mr. Silas Oakes."

"That's me." Silas took the envelope. "Thank you. Would you like a bite to eat?"

"No, thank you. I have more deliveries."

Silas sat down and opened the envelope and read:

Dear Mr. Oakes,

We regret to inform you that your wife, Mary Amelia, died last night, November the seventeenth, in the year of our Lord 1894. Cause of death is unknown. We are indeed saddened as we thought she was making progress. We await your instructions of where to send the body.

Sincerely,
J.D. Olsen, Director

The next few days were a blur. Mary Morgan Oakes wanted her delicate one buried next to the family plot in New Richmond City Cemetery. Silas took the children, accompanied by Tena, on the train from Superior to New Richmond. Levi was waiting at the station in the wagon. He hugged each girl as he boosted her up and

tickled Frank. He patted Silas on the back, "Hello, son."
He turned and shook hands with Tena, "Thank you for
coming to help."

The casket arrived on the same train. It took four men
to lift it and load it into the wagon. Levi jumped up to
the buckboard and clucked to the horses. Making conversation, Levi said, "The ground still isn't frozen, so the
grave diggers dug the grave yesterday. Your plot is just next
to ours." Silas nodded. Levi continued, "Ma arranged for
Mrs. Nelson to come wash and dress the body." Again,
Silas nodded. No one spoke as they drove to the farm.

Ma Oakes and Mrs. Nelson were waiting. Everyone
spoke in hushed tones. Ma managed a smile for the children, "Come, you must be hungry."

"I can take care of the children, Mrs. Oakes," Tena spoke
up. She bustled the children to the kitchen.

Fred and William came from the barn. They slapped
Silas on the back, mumbling condolences. Levi spoke up,
"There's a place for the casket in the parlor. We'll carry it
in through the front door." Once in place, the men pried
off the top of the pine box with hammers and wedges.
Peering inside, Silas exclaimed, "Dear God," and backed
away covering his face with his hands.

Ma approached and looked in, wailing, "Oh no, my
delicate one. They've beaten her to death." The body was
covered with deep bruises and cuts. She turned and hurried
outside to be alone.

Later, Silas found Ma sitting on a stump in Oakes
Grove, her pipe clenched in her teeth. She was white
and shaking.

He plopped down on the ground next to Mary Morgan
and buried his face in his hands. "Ma, I'm so sorry. I was
at my wit's end. I should have tried harder to keep her

home." They sat in silence for a while, then he jumped up and paced in anger, "All the rumors about asylums are true. But what can we do? They'll just deny it."

"I know you did all you could. God works in mysterious ways that we don't know. We just have to keep a stiff upper lip. Did you choose a headstone?"

"Not yet. I'll get to it later," Silas sighed, but he never did.

Back at the house, Mrs. Nelson set to work to wash the body. The task of turning the big fleshy woman took all her strength. She combed the matted hair and fashioned it into a bun. She studied the dress that was to go on. "It is just too small," she thought. She took a scissors and cut it down the back so it could be slipped on the front and tucked under. She took face powder and tried to cover the bruises on the face. She finished and opened the door and stepped into the kitchen. "It's ready," she said to those gathered there. "I'll be going now."

Reverend Walker arrived to conduct a service. Silas sat with Frank on his left and Jennie Bell and Mildred on his right. Tena sat next to Mildred and held her hand. As the minister spoke, sobs rang out. Mildred looked around frightened. She had never seen her father cry. Her grandparents and uncles, too, were crying. She whispered to Tena, "Why is everyone crying? In Sunday School, they tell us you go to heaven when you die, so why aren't they happy for Mama?"

"Because we still miss her here on earth," Tena responded.

Note

1. Mary Amelia is buried in an unmarked grave, adjacent to the Oakes family plot in New Richmond City Cemetery.

24.

"Struck it Rich"—Oakes Quarry and Mine

"I was as interested in the discovery of limestone as if it were gold."

—Henry David Thoreau

After the need for lime and rock subsided, Levi continued to dig. Old trappers' tales told of gold and silver in the bluff. On warm, summer days, when chores were done, Levi urged, "Come on boys, let's find that gold." His enthusiasm never flagged, although the boys tired of the hard labor with pickaxe and shovel.

Slowly over the next 39 years, Levi dug a mine into the cliff, shoring up the shaft with timbers. Occasionally, he found a small silver nugget. Rushing to the house, he exclaimed, "Didn't I tell you we'd find it?"

Mary Morgan just shook her head, "Well, I see you're going to be rich, Mr. Oakes." She reached to the shelf above the dry sink and took down the Mason jar with a few dime-sized nuggets. Setting the jar on the kitchen table, she lifted the wire bail holding the glass cover in place and removed the cover. Levi added another nugget to the stash.

With the help of two strong sons, Levi was free to spend more time at his mine. William, a confirmed bachelor of 27 and homebody, seemed contented working the farm. Fred, the youngest and smallest brother at 23, also remained at the home place. After eighth grade he decided he'd rather help on the farm than go to River Falls to high school. William was taller with broad shoulders and a square face, like his father, Levi. Fred was only about 5' 4" with narrow shoulders and delicate features in a triangular face, like his mother, Mary Potter. Both had light brown hair, blue eyes, but Fred sported a bushy moustache.

Levi headed past the horse barn to the mine. This day he whistled as he dug, dreaming of the nuggets he'd find. His pick struck something harder than the limestone making a metallic clink. He quickly chipped away the softer rock exposing a large chunk. He lifted it and weighed it in his hands. "Must weigh 5 pounds." Rushing out into the sunshine, he examined it closely.

Taking his pocketknife, he scraped the surface, "I think it's copper."

William, in the horse barn, was closest to the mine. He heard Pa yell and hurried out to see what was wrong. Pa was running toward the farmyard with something in his arms, shouting, "I've found it."

Fred heard the racket, hurried out of the bee house where he was gathering honeycombs.

He laughed at the sight of Pa racing across the pasture with his palsied gait. Pa slowed as William and Fred caught up with him. "Just look at this nugget. It's pure copper."

He handed it to William, who examined it. "Heavens to Betsy, you got it."

Fred took it and turned it over in his sticky hands. "I'll be a monkey's uncle."

"Get your sticky fingers off." Levi retrieved the nugget. "Whoopee!"

Mary Morgan, hearing the commotion that was loud enough to wake the dead, stepped out on the back stoop. She shaded her eyes with her hand to better see. Levi was whooping and hollering and jumping in the air. "I reckon this airy-fairy bunch has gone mad," she thought.

"I've struck it rich," Levi hollered. He reached the house and handed the chunk to her.

"That takes the cake. I reckon you haven't been on a wild goose chase all these years after all," Mary Morgan grinned as she returned the chunk of copper.

"You bet your boots I haven't," Levi retorted. He turned. "Willy, get the buggy hitched up and let's skedaddle to town," Levi commanded. "I'll show those doubting Johns. I've always felt it in my bones—there's a prize to be had in those cliffs."

Levi urged Barney into a fast trot up the hill to "Clover City," as New Richmond was affectionately called. He stopped in the general store, the pharmacy, the livery, and even the office of the St. Croix Republican.

The next week, Fred came home from town with a newspaper. "Pa, you're famous." He spread the newspaper on the kitchen table and pointed to an article. Levi and Mary Morgan peered at the paper.

"What does it say?" Levi queried.

Fred read:

Struck It Rich

"For years Mr. L.J. Oakes, residing just south of the village, has had an abiding faith that there was mineral in the

bluff along the north side of his farm, and his faith has been manifested by his works. As soon as the work on his farm was disposed of from time to time, he would resort to his task of opening his mine. And has occasionally brought to light small nuggets of silver about large enough to sweeten a cup of tea, but just before noon on Monday he found a piece of pure copper that weighed five pounds, which was shown to us during the day. What is in store in the hill, time and Mr. Oakes will reveal, and we hope he will soon strike his fortune."

St. Croix Republican, *September 11, 1893*

Although Levi continued to dig, he never found more copper. With time the mine collapsed, and the bluff eroded.

25.

Fred Moses All Grown Up

"For the hair has grown on my upper lip."
—George Orwell

"I want to meet the gal who made these swell biscuits," Fred smiled as he popped another in his mouth.

The girls by the buffet table giggled, "Hannah did," they chorused.

"Who's Hannah?"

"I am!" Hannah Andersen blushed so red all her freckles disappeared.

Fred noticed her bright red hair beautifully braided and complemented by her deep green dress. "Howdy," he grinned. "As I was saying, these are swell biscuits."

"Thank you."

They were at the Benedict's home for one of the Friday night parties for young people. Everyone looked forward to them, making the long winter more fun. They played charades and other parlor games. Whoever played an instrument joined in for singing and dancing. There were fiddles, accordions, Jew's harps, and harmonicas in addition to the piano. All the girls brought food for the midnight supper before everyone bundled up for sleigh rides home. Helping the girls serve supper, Mrs. Benedict noticed that Fred Oakes was smitten with Hannah. She smiled to herself.

After a couple of Fridays, Fred approached Hannah after the midnight supper, "May I accompany you home?"

While her girlfriends giggled, Hannah replied, "That vould be nice. I'm boarding with the Hansen's over on 2nd Street, near the Methodist Church."

"Oh, where is your family?"

"My parents have a farm near Deer Park. I'm working at O.J. Williams Dry Goods, so I stay in the village during the week."

Over the weeks Fred and Hannah became acquainted with each other and their families. "So, your parents came from Norway?" Fred inquired.

"My father is from Lenvik, and my mother from Finnsnes."

Fred laughed and teased, "Yah for sure, tell me more."

"They came in 1869. My mother never vants to be on the ocean ever again. It took four months to cross the rough, vindy Atlantic in Fall. She vas pregnant and very sick."

"You have six brothers and sisters?"

"Seven are living, but 11 counting the babies that died. My older brother, Andrew, stayed in Oregon vhen ve moved back."

"You lived in Oregon?"

"Yah, I vas about eight vhen ve went to Silverton, Oregon. Christine and Joseph vere born there. Ve came back about 1890, before Bora vas born. It is confusing because Anne and Bora are named in memory of the twins that died. The twins, plus Hans and a second Anne are buried in the Emmanuel Lutheran Cemetery in Alden Township. The current Anne is the third one."

"That must be sad for you."

"I only knew the second Anne. I was four vhen she died and didn't understand. It vas sad for my parents."

"It seems babies have a hard time getting over the diseases. I guess we're lucky to be strong and survive."

"So ve are," Hannah smiled.

April 1895

Sunday morning Fred rose early to finish his chores. After milking he headed back to the house. Inside the back door, he grabbed a gray enamel basin from the washstand and took it to the cook stove where he ladled hot water from the copper reservoir into the basin. Returning to the washstand he proceeded to lather his face and shave with the long razor, being careful to trim his moustache. He took a washcloth and scrubbed his neck and ears. After drying, he tossed the towel onto a peg on the wall. He took the stairs two at a time to his room to change. He returned to the kitchen dressed in his Sunday 'go-to-meetin' gray suit, white shirt, and black bow tie. Ma looked up from dishing out steaming bowls of oatmeal, "My, don't you look spiffy."

Fred just blushed.

Levi winked at his wife, "Do you think this one's all gussied up for Ol' Bessie?"

"His hoss don't care," chimed in William. "He's sweet on Hannah Andersen."

"As he should be," Ma retorted. "I hear she's a good catch."

Fred wolfed down the oatmeal, jumped up and carried his bowl to the sink, "Thanks, Ma. I'll be back this afternoon." He was anxious to get away from the teasing.

He took off on a run; when he was in a hurry, the horse barn seemed too far away. The horse barn was built into a bank on the north side of the creek. All the buildings were spaced about 200 feet apart, to prevent the spread of fire Pa said. Well, they'd never had a fire, but Pa sure was scared they might. Anyway, the horse barn was close to the creek and the horses were quickly watered. Bessie whinnied as Fred entered. "Good girl," he crooned. Quickly saddling her, he rode off to the Norwegian Lutheran Church near Deer Park. Arriving just as the Andersen family did, he tied Bessie to the hitchin' post and hurried over to their wagon.

Mr. Andersen tipped his hat, "Mornin', Fred."

"Good morning, it's nice to see you." He offered his hand to help Mrs. Andersen down from the wagon seat.

"Takk så mye (thanks so much)," Mrs. Andersen gave him a shy smile.

"You're very welcome."

Behind the wagon seat, two benches lined the sides of the bed for the girls to sit on, so as not to muss their Sunday dresses. It was a wagon full. Hannah was holding Bora, the two-year-old. Bora's name was really Ingeborg, but these Americans couldn't pronounce the Norwegian. They said "Inja borg." It was easier to call her Bora. Mrs. Andersen reached up and took Bora.

Joseph, now 7 years old, jumped off the back and ran to find his chums. Fred moved to the rear of the wagon and offered his hand to each girl: Christine, the impish red-headed 10-year-old; Albertine (Bertie) was shy at 12;

Anna Joanna, trying to be solemn and grownup at 14; and finally, Hannah, 19. While the family moved toward the church, Fred and Hannah lingered by the wagon.

Inside the church, Fred fidgeted, his fingers entwined and tapping, as the sermon seemed especially long. He felt Hannah's eyes on him, but he dared not look at her, his heart was pounding so. Instead, he stared at the cross on the wall behind the pulpit trying to understand the Norwegian. Finally, the last "Amen" was said, and they were free; the children rushed outside to play tag. The neighbors chatted. "These Lutherans are sure different," Fred thought. At the Methodist Church where his family went, children were disciplined to sit still and quiet on the Lord's Day.

* * *

During the spring and summer, Fred and Hannah didn't see each other as much. There was work from dawn 'til dusk on the farms. Plowing, planting, cultivating, in addition to caring for the animals. During lambing, Fred and William took bedrolls to the sheep barn to be available to assist any ewe. Fred was also making beehives. He loved honey and wanted to increase their supply. He wanted the hives ready when a swarm of bees left an old hive.

Occasionally, Hannah would visit for a few days to help Mary Morgan who was feeling her age with a touch of rheumatism. It was especially helpful on Mondays, which were laundry days. After breakfast, Fred helped Hannah drag the big iron pot out to the fire pit and set it on the limestone bricks that Levi had made years ago. Once in place, Hannah filled the pot with water from the well. Fred started the fire underneath the pot, "That should do it." He waved as he headed for the field.

Hannah fetched the wooden tubs from the shed. They were made from a barrel cut in half. She set the tubs near the pot and got buckets of water to fill them.

Mary Morgan came with baskets of dirty clothes. These she sorted into piles of whites, light colors, dark colors, and denim work clothes—the order for washing. She turned to Hannah, "Could you get the soap? It's still on the stove."

"Oh, yah." Hannah ran to the kitchen where the homemade lye soap was melting in a pan on the cook stove. She returned with the soap and ladled some into the pot and stirred it with the laundry stick, a wooden stick about a yard long, smooth, and bleached white from many washings. The tubs of water were for prewashing and rinsing. Starting with the whites, the linens were soaked and sloshed in the tub. Any stubborn stains were rubbed with soap and scrubbed against the washboard, a piece of corrugated metal with a wooden frame. When the water in the pot was boiling, the clothes were stirred in and boiled for 10-20 minutes. Clean water was put in the tubs. Hannah remembered, "Oh, I brought something for us to try; just a minute." She went back to the house and returned with a jar with a woman's face on the label, Mrs. Wright's Bluing.

"My ma got this at the general store. It's new and it's supposed to keep the linens snowy white. All you have to do is add a little to the rinse water."

"Humph! Sounds like a waste if you ask me," Mary Morgan shook her head.

"Let's try it. I'll just pour a little into the tub."

Mary Morgan watched as Hannah added the indigo liquid to the rinse water and stirred it. Then she fished the bed linens out of the pot with the laundry stick, holding them up to drain, no easy task for one as short as she.

Standing on her tip toes she was 5 feet tall. Attached to the barrel was a hand wringer to wring the linens into the blue water. When they cooled, she sloshed them up and down a few times, then rung them through the wringer, and hung them over the clothesline.

When the process was done and the tubs turned over to dry, Hannah sighed, "That's a good job done. Come, sit in the rocker on the porch and I'll get us a spot of tea."

Mary Morgan nodded, "Oh, thank you."

Hannah brought a tray with the teapot, two cups and saucers, spoons, milk, and honey. She poured the tea and sat in a chair next to Mary Morgan. "I read in Goddard's Ladies Magazine that this is what you should do after laundry. Just enjoy the tea, rock, and count your blessings."

Mary Morgan reached over and patted Hannah's hand, "You are a blessing; thank you for helping. These old bones just aren't so good anymore."

26.

Winter Weddings

"Falling in love was the easy part, planning a wedding—yikes!"
—Niecy Nash Betts

Hannah was a frequent visitor at the Oakes farm. Although she often planned to stay only a few days, snowstorms intervened and she was there for a couple of weeks. Ma was glad for the help. "When are you two gonna' get hitched?" Ma asked one evening as they sat by the stove.

Hannah dropped her knitting and blushed. She looked at Fred for help.

"Well, Ma, what makes you think we're gonna?" Fred's eyes twinkled. He loved to tease, just like his pa.

"Oh, go on with ya. It's obvious you two should get married," Ma laughed.

"How about next week?" Fred turned to Hannah.

"Fred Moses, are you proposing?" Hannah tried to sound indignant.

"Of course, if you don't want to…" Fred's voice trailed off.

"Vellllll, I'll have to give it some thought," Hannah teased.

"Gal, just say yes," Levi boomed. "You know we all want you in our family."

Soon they were all laughing and planning. "I must go home to get ready," Hannah announced. "Please, take me first thing in the morning."

Hannah's news caused a flurry of activity in the Andersen household. Anna, now 15, was left in charge of the younger siblings (Bertie, 13; Christine, 11; Joseph, 8; and Bora, 3), while Hannah and her mother, Jorgina, hurried off to purchase fabric for a wedding dress. At O.J. Williams Dry Goods, they found the perfect deep green brocade. "Dats a goot color for you," Jorgina nodded as Hannah held up the fabric. The green set off her flaming red hair.

They hurried home to sew. They arrived at the Andersen farm just as Fred rode up. "It's all arranged. Reverend Snodgrass is available next Thursday afternoon and Mr. and Mrs. Gust Phillips will stand up for us."

"You vork fast. Come in and varm yourself," Jorgina smiled. Privately she suppressed the thought of a Norwegian Lutheran service. She knew a woman follows her husband and goes to his church. So, a Methodist wedding it would be.

The kitchen was cozy and warm with the kettle singing on the stove. Joseph launched himself across the room to play fight with Fred. Jacob, Hannah's father, came in from the barn. He slapped Fred on the back, "Congratulations, young fella."

The week passed quickly. Anna helped Hannah sew while Bertie helped her ma make the Kransekake. The almonds were boiled to remove the skins, dried and ground several times to make a fine flour, then mixed with confectioner's sugar and beaten egg whites to make a paste. The paste was rolled out into "snakes" to be formed into rings in the special kransekake pans Jorgina had brought from Norway. There were 18 pans, the largest for the base was about 15 inches in diameter. Each pan was slightly smaller so the baked rings could be stacked to make a cone. The cone was drizzled with frosting and decorated with little Norwegian flags and wrapped candies on toothpicks.

Thursday, February 13, 1896, dawned bright and clear. The Andersen's were up early to finish morning chores, load everyone and food into the wagon and head for Oakes Grove. Hannah's dress was finished and wrapped in muslin to keep it clean. Several wagons were already parked by the Oakes house. Fred and William came out to help carry supplies into the house. Peeking out from under the buffalo robe, little Bora sang out, "Fred, carry me."

"Come here, baby," Fred reached for her and hoisted her from the wagon. He still hadn't been able to greet Hannah in the hubbub.

Ma Oakes was busy in the kitchen with several neighbor women who came to help. She limped to the door to greet the Andersen's. "Hello, hello. Do come in. Hannah, you, and your sisters can go up to our bedroom to change."

Two o'clock came and everyone was seated in the parlor. Fred was handsome in his new dark blue suit with a black bow tie. His moustache was neatly trimmed, and his hair freshly cut short. He stood to the left of Reverend Snodgrass with Gust Phillips. On the pastor's right stood Mrs. Phillips. Mrs. Olsen played the Wedding March on the piano for Hannah to descend from the bedroom on the arm of her father to stand in front of the wedding party. She was radiant. The green brocade dress was perfect. It had a fitted bodice with pin tucks down the front. The puffed sleeves were buttoned at the wrists with jet-black buttons. A simple white linen, removable collar accented the neckline. The ankle-length skirt was full of tiny pleats. She wore a small cameo pin at the neck. Her long red hair was combed back and neatly rolled into a bun.

A few days after the wedding, Fred sat down to write a note to his brother, Silas (S.P.), in Superior to inform him of his marriage. A couple of weeks later, he received a letter from S.P. It was the letter he had sent with some changes:

Dear ~~S.P.~~ Fred,

   Well, ol' man, we did it. ~~Hannah Andersen~~ Christina Johnson and I were married Feb. 13th at home.

                              Sincerely, ~~Fred~~ S.P.

Fred threw aside the letter, "Well if he doesn't like it, he doesn't have to."

Hannah picked up the letter and read it a couple of times, frowning. Then she laughed, "I think S.P. and Tena were married the same day." Another family joke. Sixty-three years later, Fred and Hannah's grandson Bruce married Alcie Smith, February 13, 1959.

Note

1. Several Oakes men were known by their initials.

27.

A New Generation at Oakes Grove

"The soil is the great connector of lives."
—Wendell Berry

"Hannah, welcome to our home. We're right glad Fred married such a good woman. We hope you'll stay here. With Silas and Charlie movin' their families all the way up to Superior and William such a confirmed bachelor, it's too goldarn quiet here," Ma Oakes smiled at Hannah.

"Of course, that will be fine," Hannah replied.

Ma suggested, "I think the newlyweds should have our room." It was the larger bedroom upstairs on the southeast corner. The east window looked toward the outbuildings and horse barn along Paper Jack Creek. The south window looked across Paper Jack Creek to the fields, now snow covered but blooming with clover in summer. The room was simple. The bed was handmade of oak boards covered with a straw tick, muslin sheets and a quilt that Ma had made. The piecework of the quilt top was fashioned from sewing scraps into a God's Eye pattern in random bright hues. The wool batting was from last year's sheep shearing. Instead of fancy quilt stitching, it was tied with yarn every 4 inches, giving the quilt a puffy look.

"Oh, we don't want to inconvenience you, Ma," Hannah insisted.

"It's no trouble. I've been thinking we should move downstairs. My ol' bones just don't fancy the climb anymore."

Levi smiled, his eyes twinkling, "I have to do what Ma says. You see she's older than me."

William and Fred moved things around. The small bedroom next to the other room became Pa and Ma's bedroom; although small, there was room for a bed, dresser, and a chair next to the chamber pot. Wooden pegs along the wall provided room to hang overalls, shirts, dresses, and nightgowns.

Fred and Hannah moved into the larger bedroom upstairs. Hannah unpacked the quilt she made and laid it on the bed. She ran her hands over the quilt, admiring the fine stitches on the log cabin design. Each square was composed of small squares of red and white or blue and white fabrics sewn together so that reds were on one side of the square, blue on the other with a white center. The squares were sewn together so that stripes of red, white, and blue emerged diagonally across the quilt.

The second upstairs bedroom remained for William.

* * *

"Surely is a comfort to have another woman in the house," Ma sank wearily into a chair as she smiled at Hannah. They had just finished the dinner dishes.

"Why, thank you," Hannah smiled back and then frowned. "You look tired. Why don't you go lie down for a spell?"

"I reckon that's a good idea."

All fall Ma grew frailer. On October 16, 1896, she died. Levi sat by her bedside all morning. "Pa, come to dinner," Fred gently urged.

Levi just shook his head, "I'll sit here 'till they come to prepare the body. Then I'll go make a coffin. That seems to be my lot in life. How many have I made?" he asked bitterly, of no one in particular.

Fred patted him on the shoulder, "I'll help."

"NO!" Levi rose and headed for the back door. In the machine shed, he got a ladder to pull boards from the rafters. From the oaks cut last year there were fine straight boards. In spite of himself, he chuckled, "Mary Morgan Oakes will be buried in an oak box." As he worked, he thought of the other coffins he'd built: his first love, Mary Potter; Fred's twin dying at birth; son Albion—just 19; his old friend Ed Johnson; and now his beloved Mary Morgan. "How many more will God take and expect me to build their coffins?" With only the cows to hear, Levi sobbed.

All the family gathered for the funeral. Sons Silas and Charlie came from Superior with their wives and children. Even though Mary Morgan was their stepmother, they loved her dearly. They reminisced about how she had astounded them by smoking a pipe. "Remember how the ashes dropped in our food?" Charlie roared with laughter.

It was evident that Hannah was pregnant, making the day more jovial. Tena squeezed Hannah's hand, "I'm so happy for you. Life goes on."

Silas clapped Fred on the back, "Congratulations, ol' chap."

"It'll be a joy to have a rug rat again," Levi chuckled, observing Hannah's bulging stomach.

"I hope you'll say that when it keeps you up at night," Hannah laughed, rubbing her expanding belly. Esther Luella made her debut on a blustery morning, March 11, 1897.

Soon spring planting of corn, oats, and barley consumed the men folk. Hannah managed all the household—cleaning, laundry, cooking, baking—all with Esther in a basket nearby. She tended the chickens and planted the vegetable garden, using seeds she had ordered from the new Mr. Burpee's Flower and Vegetable Seeds catalog. "So different and modern," she mused, "to make an order and send it by post with a check from the bank instead of going to the feed store."

Fred and William returned from two days of getting the crops in over at Ed Johnson's place in Cylon. Ed had deeded his 40 acres to Levi in exchange for Levi and Mary Morgan caring for him in his old age. When he could no longer farm, Fred and William took care of the farm. He died in 1880 and was buried in the Oakes family plot in City Cemetery. Ever since, the boys kept that farm going.

As they sat down to dinner, Levi inquired, "Ya finish the corn plantin'?"

"Sure thing, Pa," Fred nodded. "We've been thinkin' that Hannah and I should move over there. The old farmhouse needs some work, but it's livable. Farmin' would be easier if we lived there. You and William can handle this place."

Levi leaned back in his chair and eyed Hannah, "That alright with you?"

"Yah, fer sure, it'll be an adventure," Hannah laughed.

By July, the farmhouse was patched up and scrubbed, so Fred loaded up the wagon with their belongings, Hannah, and baby Esther.

Levi walked through the quiet house, remarking to William, "Sure is quiet with just us bachelors."

28.

A Perfect Day for a Circus

"Word gets around when the circus comes to town, don't it?"
—Cormac McCarthy

Hannah woke to the rooster crowing at first light. She stretched and remembered today is the circus. The flyers had been up for weeks—Gollmar Brothers Circus coming to New Richmond on June 12, 1899. She smiled and quickly rose to use the chamber pot and splash water on her face from the commode basin. Brushing and braiding her flaming red hair was done in a flash. She pulled on her undergarments and blue gingham work dress. Peeking out the window, she saw the sunrise, brilliant yellows, and pinks, without a cloud in the sky. "Perfect day for a circus, Fred."

Fred was still snoring, so she shook him, "Mornin' sleepy head. Time to fly so we don't miss the parade."

Popping out of bed, he grabbed her arm and spun her around, "Yes siree, we're off to the circus." He hurriedly dressed and headed to the barn for milking.

First, Hannah started the fire in the cook stove so the kettle would heat for coffee. Time to get the children up. Esther, now 27 months, could partly dress herself while

Hannah dressed baby Art. At 11 months, he was walking and babbling. "Esther, today is the circus. Ve'll take a picnic lunch, vatch the parade, and see the circus."

"Ma, what animals will be there?" Esther asked, as she tugged at her dress.

"Oh, elephants, lions, acrobatic dogs, and Minnie the smallest pony in the vorld, they say."

"Can I ride Minnie?"

"No, ve'll yust vatch. I think she does tricks."

Fred finished milking, carried the full milk cans to the icehouse, hitched ole Jack to the wagon and drove it up to the house. Glancing skyward, he remarked, "Hannah, just look at this perfect day—not a cloud in the sky." There was no sign of what would unfold by nightfall.

"Yah, it'll be goot for the circus, but maybe a touch too hot. It already feels humid."

"I suppose you could leave off your petticoat," Fred teased.

"Posh, go on with ya." Hannah playfully slapped him on the shoulder. They all changed into their dress clothes.

Living on Ed Johnson's farm in Cylon Township, they were about 8 miles from New Richmond. As they approached town, more wagons and buggies filled the road. People waved and called, "Great day for a circus." Main Avenue was lined with carts, wagons, buggies, bicycles, and lots of people.

"Looks like the population has doubled," Fred declared. "After the worst winter in years, everyone is anxious to get out."

"Yah, I don't vant to go through another vinter like that. Sixty below zero and 5 feet of snow vas too much," Hannah replied.

"Let's try to park the wagon near the circus grounds in the shade for Jack," Fred directed.

"Here's a goot place." Hannah pointed to a spot by a giant cottonwood.

Fred tied Jack to a tree and set the child's red wagon on the ground. Hannah added a folded homespun blanket and set the children in it. Pulling the wagon, they joined the crowds lining the street. They could hear the brass and reed bands heralding the parade.

Soon one of the bands was in front of them, followed by a clown slapping his feet in oversized duck-like shoes. His face was painted white with a crimson nose. With his megaphone, he shouted, "Ladies and Gentlemen and young'uns too, you are about to see the leading show in the world. Gollmar Brothers have a monster menagerie for your entertainment. Here comes Palm, the Grand Heroic War Elephant."

Spectators clapped and shouted. For many it was the first elephant they'd seen. Palm was followed by horse-drawn wagons with cages of lions, a leopard, and bears. Another clown lifted his megaphone and announced, "Herr Drayton, the German giant of strength, the Sampson of the 19th Century." The tall, stocky, red-haired German was indeed a giant with bulging muscles.

"Oh, look," Hannah pointed, "there's Minnie." The black miniature pony was daintily prancing along with her trainer.

"Goldarn, I've never seen such a small pony," Fred shook his head.

Another brass and reed band brought up the rear of the parade. People fell in line behind and followed into the big top. As the afternoon wore on, getting hotter and hotter, baby Art grew fussy. Hannah loosened his shirt and tried to rock him on her knee. She nursed him and he fell asleep. All around people were fanning themselves with newspapers, hankies, or fans. One man poured a cup of water over his head.

Just as the circus ended, rain and hail poured down. Everyone lingered, waiting for a break. As it eased, Fred grabbed up Esther, "Let's go." Hannah put Art in the red wagon and raced to the buckboard. Other farm folk rushed by. It was time to get home for evening chores–if they were late, the cows would be bawling to be milked.

The ancient cottonwood trees arching overhead blocked the rain and the sky. Fred urged Jack to a trot. "I don't like this." Out of town they reached a clearing where they saw the sky to the southwest was an eerie green.

"Have you ever seen such a sky?" Hannah queried.

"Can't say I have. Best we get home."

Both were relieved to reach the farmyard. Jack whinnied and shook his head. Hannah hurried inside with the children. "Strange there is no breeze at all," she though. "Come Esther, ve'll change out of our goot dresses."

"Mama, I so hot. Don't want a dress."

"All right, stay in your petticoat." Changing back into her blue gingham dress, she giggled, blushed, and left off her petticoat.

Art's damp hair was plastered to his head and rivulets of perspiration ran down by his ears. Hannah stripped off his clothes and sponged him with a wet washcloth. "I reckon you can stay in your diaper."

"Come, ve'll get supper." Just as they entered the kitchen, Hannah glanced at the clock. "Six o'clock, already." There was a loud rumbling as if a freight train were in the yard. Hannah rushed outside. Fred heard it, too, and ran out of the barn. Above the trees to the southwest, they saw the black clouds roiling upwards with huge strikes of lightening.

"Quick, take the children to the cellar. It must be a cyclone," Fred shouted.

Scooping up Art and taking Esther by the hand, Hannah ran to the root cellar and lifted the door. The cellar was dug into the ground about 5 feet. It was covered with boards and heaped with dirt. She hurried down the wooden stairs and set Art on the dirt floor. She took candles off a shelf, placed them in holders and lit them. Running back up the stairs, she grabbed the rope on the door and pulled it down. The sudden darkness caused both children to whimper. They stared at their mother with wide frightened eyes. "Now, now, isn't this fun?" Hannah soothed. "Oh, it is so nice and cool."

The cellar door partly lifted on its hinges and Fred held it as he descended, letting the door close. "It looks bad out there."

To distract the children, they played pat-a-cake and sang. It was so quiet; they didn't know what was happening outside. After about half an hour, Fred cautiously raised the door; it was calm. "I think the coast is clear." He climbed out, turned, and took Art. Esther and Hannah followed. They stood and surveyed the sky. Gray clouds rolled overhead. Suddenly, a gale blew out of the northwest, ripping leaves off trees, scattering pails, and other small things. They turned and hurried back down into the cellar.

Ten minutes seemed an eon before they again peaked out. This time, only puffy white clouds floated by, and the wind died down. The yard was filled with debris; "It vill take all day to clean up this mess," Hannah wailed.

Putting his arm around her, Fred comforted, "But we're safe."

"So, ve are. I yust have to count my blessings," Hannah hugged Art and Esther. "Come, ve'll have some supper."

Fig. 3 Gollmar Bros. Circus Advertisement

29.

Cyclone, 1899

*"...such a severe winter—wait patiently for summer,
and summer came and brought us death."*

—Anna Epley, 1899, New Richmond

The rooster crowed, though it was barely light. Fred and Hannah were dressing. Best to start the day early. It promised to be another scorcher. They needed to see the damage from last night's storm, plus it was milking time.

Unaware of the disaster in New Richmond, Fred finished milking and turned the cows out to pasture. He whistled for his sheepdog, Duke, and they checked on the sheep placidly grazing in the south pasture. They returned to the house. Entering the back stoop washroom, Fred called, "Hannah, it's going to be another hot, humid day." He took off his barn shoes and slipped on his house shoes. Next to the small window stood the commode with a china washbowl and water pitcher. Next to the washbowl was a plate with homemade lye soap. Fred scrubbed his hands and washed his face. After drying his hands and face, he carried the washbowl outside and threw the water on Hannah's flower bed by the back door. He smiled. Hannah loved the hollyhocks blooming there. In the kitchen, Fred's favorite breakfast was ready: oatmeal with honey and cream, plus fresh bread and sweet butter.

Just as they were finishing, they heard a galloping horse. "Hello! Hello!" Rushing to the door, they saw a sweaty, young man on a lathered horse, swarming with flies. "Help is needed. The cyclone destroyed New Richmond. If you've got a pair of strong draft horses, come at once. We need to move timbers to get at the injured. Take the south road. The north bridge over Willow River is gone." He waved and galloped off.

Too stunned to ask questions, they stared after the rider. They exclaimed in unison, "Oh, Pa and William...."

"I'd better go there first to see if they're alright," Fred pulled on his boots and ran to the barn to hitch the team to the wagon. Their farm in Cylon Township was about 8 miles from Oakes Grove, which was about a mile south of New Richmond.

"I'll get food and blankets," Hannah shouted after him. She grabbed a large basket from a hook in the washroom and hurried down the basement stairs. She gathered cheese, eggs, and jars of applesauce. Back in the kitchen she grabbed loaves of bread and took the cookie jar—just a glass gallon jar from Nash Coffee Company—filled with oatmeal cookies.

Fred was waiting in the driveway. Hannah handed the basket to him. "Wait, I'll get blankets and sheets." She hurried back into the house and returned with an armload of blankets and sheets. "Godspeed," she waved.

Approaching Oakes Grove from the southeast, Fred strained to look. Everything looked normal. At the farm he shouted, "Hallo, hallo, anybody here?" He drove to the watering trough to water the horses. He jumped down and ran to the barn. The wagon was gone. "They must be in town; nothing amiss here," he thought. Back at the wagon, he yanked the horses from the trough, "Alright, you've had enough." He clucked them to a trot north to town.

The sight of Main Avenue (now Knowles Avenue) took his breath away. "Whoa," he pulled the horses to a stop so he could survey the scene. This was worse than the fire of 1892 when half of Main Avenue was devastated. He whistled softly, "Dear God." On Main Avenue, between First and Sixth Streets, all the buildings were gone—only jumbles of splintered lumber and bricks. The giant cottonwood trees lining Main Avenue were all gone. The electric power plant was blown away. The electric, telegraph, and telephone lines lay tangled on the ground. From the southwest corner of town, the cyclone tore a 1,000-foot-wide swath across to the northeast corner (shown in Figure 4). Dead animals—horses, mules, a few cows, and chickens—littered the road. O.J. Williams Dry Goods store was a jumble of bricks, cement, and burning timbers. The sturdy brick building had seemed a refuge in the moments before the cyclone hit. Many people rushed inside and down to the basement. The twister sucked up the bricks and roof timbers and hurled them back down on the crowd huddled in the cellar. Shortly after, lightning started the timbers on fire.

Men scurried about shouting directions for hooking chains to timbers and teams of horses. "Take her away," a man shouted and waved to a driver. The horses strained, urged on by their owner. Slowly, inch-by-inch, the big timber moved. At last, it was free. But other timbers shifted. It was like a giant pile of pick-up sticks.

Fred heard moans, screams, and a dog barking. Here and there a dazed person wandered aimlessly. Smoke rose from several places along the street where fire had started, especially at O.J. Williams Dry Goods. The smell of burned wood and flesh filled the air. Gazing further north, everything had been swept away.

A man rushed up, "Come this way." He guided Fred's horses through the debris.

"Have you got any buckets?" another man inquired. "The water system is gone."

Fred shook his head; a few buckets seemed useless in this chaos. Several teams of horses were already chained to timbers. As Fred wondered where to begin, two men approached, carrying a makeshift stretcher of two boards with a blanket wrapped around them. A young woman on the stretcher was moaning softly. They laid her in Fred's wagon. "Take her to the schoolhouse. It's the temporary hospital. Dr. Epley is there."

Half of the schoolhouse was blown away. In the half still standing, Dr. Epley directed volunteers. He spotted Fred and rushed to see the patient. He called to Dr. Ward, "See to this girl." He directed Fred, "Wait. We're sending the injured to St. Paul. It's much too dirty here and we have no bandages or medicines. All four pharmacies blew away, as did part of my office. You can transport patients to the Minneapolis-Omaha train just on the tracks at 6th and Minnesota."

Fred and a volunteer carefully lifted a dazed man with a broken leg into the wagon. Behind them a voice called out, "Are you going to the train? Doc says I must go. My arm is broke."

Fred observed a plucky girl about 8 years old. Her dress was wet and dirty, and her hair matted. Mud was smeared across her face. Someone had made a sling from a flour sack tea towel for her left arm. "Where are your folks?"

"Getting hurt ones."

"What's your name?"

"Abbie."

"Alright, Abbie. Is it painful?"

"I can stand it," she replied with a grimace.

Fred gingerly placed his hands around her waist and lifted her into the wagon. "Here, lean against the sideboard."

One of the volunteers spoke up, "Time to get to the train. I'll go with you to help. By the way, I'm Jack Olsen."

"I'm Fred Oakes," he extended his hand and shook Jack's.

As they made their way, Jack filled Fred with details. "I got here about 4 this morning on the train from Hudson. When a messenger from New Richmond got to the telegraph office in Roberts, the clerk there sent out an appeal for volunteers, doctors, and medical supplies. In Hudson, a boy was sent to knock on doors. A special train was commissioned. Dear Lord Almighty, it was hell. We were trying to get to trapped victims crying out for help. That big store downtown was the worst. The building was just dumped into the cellar where people tried to shelter. We'd see arms, legs, heads sticking out. We'd get the timbers and bricks moved only to find it was just a limb or head—no body. And the fires..." he shook his head, "No way to fight fire with no water. We were helpless; I'll never forget as long as I live the screams of those burning to death. We couldn't get to them," Jack paused and held his head in his hands with elbows resting on his knees. "It's good to sit a spell," he sighed.

As they headed south on Arch Street, a swarm of mosquitoes attacked. The men swatted and waved their hands around their heads. Even the horses snorted and shook their heads. They turned west on 6th Street and saw the train tracks were a hub of activity. The hospital train was filling up. Wagons were waiting to deposit the injured.

Those most critical were laid in boxcars while those who could sit were put in coaches.

A train from Hudson pulled in. Sightseers dressed in fancy clothes alighted, laughing, and joking. The volunteers were stunned into silence.

Fred felt his face flush with anger, "Goldarn it," they ought to stay home or help."

"Yah, I heard there were looters, too," Jack nodded.

Hearing them, another man added, "I heard the Wisconsin Militia is on the way."

Fred scowled, "They can't get here any too soon."

Company C, the Tenth Battalion of the Wisconsin Militia (now the National Guard), arrived from Chippewa Falls and remained until June 29, 1899. A second train chugged to a stop amid a hiss of steam. It was full of volunteers, medical supplies, and equipment from the St. Paul Fire Department, including a water tender. A tall, blond, dapper young man in a brown suit, white shirt and brown bow tie scrambled down from the train. He was carrying a black doctor's bag. He approached Fred, "Where's the hospital?"

"Climb up, we're on our way there."

"Thanks. We need to get the supplies I brought. By the way, I'm Dr. Sorenson."

Fred and Jack helped Dr. Sorensen fill the wagon with boxes marked "Medical." All three squeezed onto the seat.

"How bad is it?" Dr. Sorensen inquired.

"We don't know for sure. The injured and dead are still being pulled out of the mess," Jack said quietly, his shoulders slumping, his eyes bulging out of his soot covered face.

By noon, the sun beat down relentlessly on the almost treeless town. The humidity, smoke and stench of rotting flesh made it hard to breathe. Fred mopped his face with his red bandana. Sweat trickled down his back. His blue muslin shirt was already soaked and sticking to his back.

At the schoolhouse a volunteer shouted to Fred and Jack, "Go back to Main Street. They need transports to take the dead. The Congregational and Catholic Churches are morgues now."

Bodies were laid out on Main Street. If scraps of clothes, sheets, or blankets were found, they covered the bodies. Most were just there in their dirty, ripped clothes, a few were naked as the force of the twister carried off their clothes. Volunteers quickly filled Fred's wagon with bodies. They headed for the Congregational Church back on Fourth Street, across from the school. Fred whistled softly. Some of the church was damaged. Pastor Adams met them. "God bless us all," he squeezed Fred's shoulder and patted Jack's back. "Just bring them to the sanctuary. Most of the main sanctuary is still there. We tore out the pews to make room to receive the dead and injured."

Late in the day, Fred spotted William with a crew clearing the street. He called, "Hey William, you alright?"

"I've been better, but no complaints."

"Where's Pa?"

"He's plumb tuckered out. He's sitting down over yonder." William pointed. "He's too old for this, but he refused to stay home."

Suddenly, Fred was overcome with fatigue; his arms ached, his legs shook, and his throat parched. "Let's take Pa home. I could use water and something to eat. I'll bring the wagon over."

Fred returned to get the wagon. "Jack, come with us. Pa's farm is just a mile south. We'll get food and water for us and the horses."

Jack hesitated, "There's still work here."

"We can come back. It'll do us good."

Jack nodded, climbed into the wagon and they drove over to Pa.

"Howdy, Pa. Time to feed and water the horses and get some grub." Fred extended his hand to help Pa get up.

"Good golly, Fred. When did you get here?"

"Oh, sometime this morning."

"Where's William?" Pa asked.

"He's getting your team and wagon to follow us."

With the mess on Main Street, they drove down Arch Street and returned to Main Street on the south side of town. There the damage ended. They marveled at the straight line of destruction. The cyclone had come from the Southwest hitting town about Fifth and Minnesota. It continued Northeast in a swath about 1,000 feet wide, wiping out all the business district and residences all the way north to the Willow River and beyond.

"How is it over at Cylon?" Pa inquired.

"There are some trees down and lots of limbs. When we got word of New Richmond early this morning, I came at once. I stopped by the farm; looks like Oakes Grove is fine."

Pa replied, "Maybe. We haven't seen it in daylight. Last night we got asked to bring water. William and I filled milk cans and buckets and hauled it to town. This is the worst storm I've ever seen. We heard the roar and headed for the root cellar. The wind was fierce. And such a strange green light in the sky. Looking up towards town we saw houses, trees, horses, people sucked up and dumped. Then whirled upwards again. It was barely over when a north-west wind howled down with pelting rain for over an hour," Pa wrung his hands and slumped.

"Yah, I noticed all the mud. Even if debris was cleared, the muddy streets slowed the horses. They sank to their knees in some places," Fred said.

At the farm, Levi jumped down from the wagon. "I'll rustle up some grub," Levi called as he headed into the house.

Fred unhitched the horses at the watering trough. "There, they may graze while we eat," Fred nodded to no one in particular.

Soon William arrived and followed suit with his team. The three men pumped water at the well, sticking their heads under the cold, refreshing liquid. Shaking off and wiping their hands on their overalls, they headed to the house. Levi had set out bread, butter, cheese, a pitcher of milk, a jar of canned tomatoes, and a pot of coffee. "Come on, boys, you must be starved." They ate in silence, too exhausted from the horror of the day for conversation.

"We need to get back to town," William offered. "Pa, why don't you stay home?"

"Well, someone needs to milk the cows," Levi stated.

* * *

The next day, Fred returned to Cylon. Hannah questioned him, "How was it?"

Fred just shook his head and sighed, "Later. I need to see how much damage there is here." He unhitched the team of horses from the wagon and turned them loose in the pasture.

Hannah and Fred eagerly read The Republican each day for news of deaths and funerals and other developments. The final death toll was 117 and 200 injured. The newspaper reported the outpouring of aid. Governor Scofield called on neighboring counties to provide aid. He appointed banks to collect the funds. The Republican reported as funds accumulated from many groups: Commercial Club of St. Paul, Odd Fellows, Modern Woodman, The German-American Red Cross Society of St. Paul, towns of Morris, Minnesota and Boyd, Wisconsin. A total of $137,406 was collected.

With volunteers and aid pouring in, most of Main Avenue was rebuilt in five months. Some businessmen set up temporary buildings to carry on. The mangled and twisted iron bridge over the Willow River was sent on a flatbed railroad car to Chicago where it was straightened. It was returned and reinstalled. Two prominent women of the community, Anna Epley and Mrs. A.G. Boehm, published memories of the cyclone.

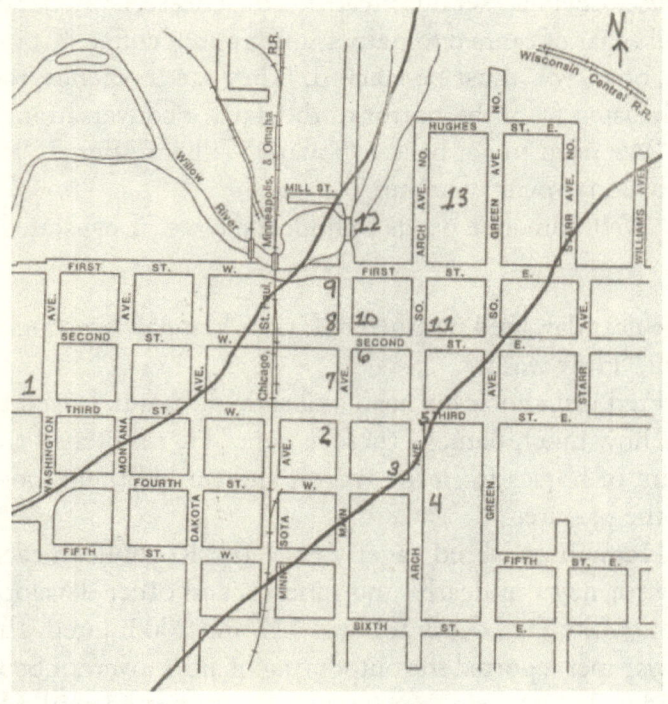

Fig. 4 Approximate Path of Cyclone, June 12, 1899*

*From *Monthly Weather Review*, July 1899, in *Intensive Survey Report*, New Richmond, WI, June 1983.

PI = Claudette Stager, City of New Richmond.

Building key on Map added by author, Kay Oakes Oring, from multiple accounts of the cyclone:

1-Catholic Church

2-OJ Williams Dry Goods

3-Congregational Church

4-School

5-Dr. Epley's office and home

6-Telephone & Post Office

7-Bank of New Richmond

8-Manufacturer's Bank

9-Nicoletter Hotel

10-Farmer's Hotel

11-Methodist Church

12-Bridge blown away

13-all houses on block lifted and smashed

30.

Back to Oakes Grove

"Home is where love resides, memories are created, friends and family belong, and laughter never ends."

—Unknown

Fred and Hannah worked hard, and the farm at Cylon prospered. By summer 1900, another baby, Florence Evangeline, made her debut.

The following summer, their neighbor, Frank Jones, rode up on his handsome Morgan horse. "Mornin', Fred." He dismounted and shook hands. "Your oats are comin' along mighty fine."

"Yah, the rain helped," Fred agreed. He took the straw stem he was chewing out of his mouth and continued, "What can I do for ya?"

"I was wonderin' if you might consider sellin' your place? I'd like to add it to mine."

Fred scratched his head, "Well…I can't rightly say as it belongs to my Pa."

After discussions and negotiations, Levi sold. Fred and Hannah with their growing brood Esther (4), Art (3), and Florence (1) moved back to Oakes Grove.

"Welcome home," Levi boomed as he set Art down from the wagon and grinned at Hannah.

"Maybe you won't be so happy when we fill up your house," Hannah joked.

"No, no, young'uns make a home. It's mighty fine to have ya back. The house was too quiet," Levi beamed as he reached to tussle Art's hair.

A couple of cots were added to Fred and Hannah's bedroom upstairs. Esther and Florence shared one with their heads at opposite ends. Art had the other cot. In January they added a cradle for the baby expected any day now. That cold January 21, 1902, Ardis Geneva arrived to ohs and ahs of the family. Hannah's sister, Anne, came to help for a few days. Hannah seemed so tired. She complained of pain. On the third day she developed a fever and could barely sit up.

Anne came from the kitchen with a bowl of steaming chicken soup. "This should help you feel better," she announced as she set the bowl on the pine table next to the bed. She helped Hannah sit up and held the bowl of soup while Hannah took a few bites. Fred Moses hurried through the morning chores and returned to the house to sit with his suffering wife.

Levi entered the bedroom quietly. Putting his hand on Fred's shoulder, he whispered, "Come down for dinner."

Reluctantly, Fred followed. William got the children settled at the table. Anne served the meal of pork pot roast, potatoes, onions, and rutabagas. They ate silently. Fred sighed, "What should I do?"

"Send for the doctor," Levi advised.

William offered, "I'll go."

William returned with Dr. Epley who went at once to see Hannah in the upstairs bedroom. "You have childbed fever," he declared.

Hannah gasped, "Oh, no." She covered her mouth with her hand.

"We'll get you treated," the good doctor replied. He called down the stairs, "Miss Andersen, please come here."

Anne ran up the stairs. "What do you need?'

Taking a small vial from his bag, he handed it to Anne, "This is tincture of aconite. Put two drops in a glass of water for Hannah to drink morning and night. Do not give her any more of it. It should bring the fever down." He took a bottle of carbonic acid out of his bag. "Now we need some clean cloths—some that can be ripped up."

"I'll get them," Anne called over her shoulder as she hurried away. She returned with several pieces of muslin.

Dr. Epley tore off a wide strip. "We'll soak this with carbonic acid and bathe her bottom area. Do it several times a day. If there is pus, wash her with soap and water." He pulled a chair to the bedside and took Hannah's hand, "Drink lots of fluids. Eat small meals with scalded milk."

Hannah asked, "What about the baby? Will she get it?"

"I don't think so. She should be fine." He rose and went to the cradle where Ardis was sleeping. "She looks fine. I won't disturb her." He returned to the bedside, "Mrs. Oakes, you're a strong young woman. That will do you well." Turning to Anne, he said, "I think you'll do fine as her nurse. Send for me if you need."

Downstairs he sat down with the men folk. "She has childbed fever." He paused, then went on, "I've given Miss Andersen instructions for her care. Mrs. Oakes is a strong young woman. That will do her well." He rose, "I must be going." He shook Fred's hand.

"Thank you," Fred mumbled. Then blurted out, "What can I ever do without her?" He knew childbed fever was often a death sentence.

"God willing, she'll pull through," Dr. Epley replied.

The next days were a blur for Fred. At night when Ardis cried, he got up, changed her diaper, and took her to the bed for Hannah to nurse. Anne took care of her and cooked. Levi and William played with the children and took them sledding.

On the sixth day, the fever broke, and Hannah sat up and ate all her dinner. "I am feeling a bit better." She smiled at Fred, "I think I've made it." They held each other and wept.

Hannah's recovery was rapid, and Ardis were thriving. Soon Hannah was back to her laughing, energetic self. She propped her Bible and hymn book on a chair in front of her spinning wheel, so she read or sang as she spun, following her own mother's example.

Watching, Esther inquired, "Ma, how do you do that?"

Hannah looked up from her Bible, "Vat?"

"Spin without looking."

"Oh, I yust feel the vool. Come, sing with me," she invited as she exchanged the Bible for the hymnal. Soon the other young'uns gathered and joined them.

Beside her chair in the parlor was a basket of handiwork. After dinner she sat a spell and picked up the latest project—knitting socks and mittens; embroidering pillowcases and matching dresser scarves; crocheting doilies, tablecloths, or collars to perk up a dress; or piecing quilt squares.

The men folk also usually rested after dinner before they headed out for an afternoon of farm work. Levi smiled as he sat up from his cat nap on the floor. He smiled at Hannah, "I do declare girl, you never rest."

Hannah laughed, "This is rest." As her daughters grew, she taught them these skills. They all liked counted cross stitch in the Scandinavian tradition.

Note

1. The childbirth fever incident was recounted in a poem for Fred and Hannah:

    But God spared her to them for he knew her great worth
    To her husband and wee helpless babes,
    There was much to be done on this great, busy earth
    So this good mother's life it was saved.

    From *The Golden Wedding, A tribute to Fred & Hannah Oakes on their Fiftieth Anniversary* by Eleanor Espelien (sister of their daughter-in-law, Lillian Oakes, wife of Fred Arthur). The entire poem is included in Appendix I.

2. Hannah's spinning wheel and some of her handspun knitted socks are in the New Richmond Heritage Center, New Richmond, WI.

31.

Diphtheria

"The Strangler"

—common name for diphtheria

Levi and Fred were in town to pick up seed corn for spring planting. As they drove the horses and wagon down Main Street, Dr. Epley hailed them. "Good morning, Fred. How is Hannah?"

Fred grinned, "Fit as a fiddle."

"And how are your young'uns?"

"Growin' like weeds," Fred chuckled.

"There's been an outbreak of diphtheria. Bring your little ones in for shots. It's best to protect them with this new vaccine."

"I'll tell Hannah, but she is pretty opposed to it," Fred responded.

"Have her talk to me. Diphtheria is such a dreadful death."

"We'll see. Thanks for telling us."

Arriving at home, Fred drove the wagon to the barn where William was repairing a harness. He jumped up to help unload the wagon. When they were finished, William said, "I'll stable the horses, go ahead up to the house for dinner."

Soon they were seated around the table. Levi was at the head of the table, smiling at his brood. Hannah bustled around getting three-year-old Art settled on a chair with two Sears Roebuck catalogs to boost him up. She asked, "Esther, please get Florence into her highchair."

The guys took their places on the sides. Hannah sat at the other end of the table, nearest the kitchen. She passed the ham with raisin sauce, scalloped potatoes, canned corn from last fall's harvest, pickles, fresh bread, and butter.

"When do you think the fields will be dry enough to plow?" Levi asked.

"Maybe by next week, unless it rains," William replied.

Fred interjected, "Hannah, we saw Dr. Epley in town. He said we should bring the young'uns to his office to get shots to prevent diphtheria. There's been an outbreak."

"Humph! Over my dead body," Hannah retorted. "They get that stuff from horses. No vay is anyone going to put it in my children."

William chimed in, "I heard people in town say Dr. Epley should be shot for telling everyone to get vaccinated."

"Yah, ya betcha," Hannah nodded.

"Now wait," Levi said. "Dr. Epley is an educated man. He must know it's alright."

"It can't be goot to put horse serum into people. I heard that young'uns have died from those shots," Hannah exploded.

"But children die from diphtheria," Levi cautioned.

"Ve'll yust keep them home," Hannah said firmly. She railed against vaccines all her life. None of her eight children, or the two nephews whom they raised, were vaccinated. They were lucky as none contracted diphtheria.

Notes

1. Horses do not become ill from diphtheria but develop antibodies to it. The serum may be extracted and used to inject into people. There were cases of a few children dying after receiving the vaccine. It was found that the particular horse had typhus which was carried in the serum. After that, typhus serum was added along with the diphtheria serum.

2. Hannah's son, Hollis, accepted his mother's opposition to vaccines. He refused to allow his son and older daughter, Kay (the author) to be vaccinated until she almost died from whooping cough. After that his wife put down her foot, "These kids will be vaccinated."

32.

Another Family at Oakes Grove

"Generational transitions are filled with opportunities."
—Hana Ben-Shabat

Hannah was the first to notice the change in William. He was acting like a young colt, prancing around as he went about his day, whistling and singing. On Friday night he washed and shaved and got all slicked up in his white shirt and brown tweed Sunday-go-to-meetin' suit and announced, "I'm going to town." At first no one commented, but this behavior continued every Friday.

"Who's the lady?" Fred teased.

William blushed scarlet and mumbled, "No one."

"Ho, ho, William's gone sweet on a gal. Come on. Out with it," Levi demanded playfully. Even Esther joined the fun, "Uncle William, do you have a gal?"

"Ya know, I hear William's been at the young people's socials on Friday nights," Hannah added, her eyes twinkling.

"Where'd you hear that?" William floundered, still blushing. "Alright, so I have. What of it?"

Fred pushed, "Your strange new behavior must mean a lady. Come on, don't just sit there like a bump on a log."

William fumbled with the button on his suit, "Hannah, I've been thinkin', is it alright if I bring her to dinner Sunday?"

"Yah, ya betcha," Hannah grinned. "Does she have a name?"

"Myrtle...Myrtle Moon," William blushed again.

"Bully for you," Fred slapped him on the back.

The romance flourished and they were married the next summer, 1902. The old house was filled. By spring 1903, both Hannah and Myrtle were with child.

"I think we need to add a utility room on to the back of the kitchen," Levi observed. "There's goin' be a heap of washing."

The men folk built a fine room including a new stove with an oversized reservoir to heat water, stands for new washtubs with a drain to the outside and a new-fangled washing machine. It had a hand crank to agitate the clothes and a hand wringer. Clotheslines were strung across the back behind the stove for drying clothes in winter. When finished, they brought Myrtle and Hannah to see its wonders.

"Yust look at dat!" Hannah exclaimed. "Dat looks mighty goot."

"It will make laundry day easier," Myrtle agreed.

33.

A Surprise for Hannah

"The husband who decides to surprise his wife is often very much surprised himself."

—Voltaire

Fred Moses stepped off the buckboard and surveyed the fields with a sense of satisfaction: spring planting was done. Life could be more leisurely until the corn, barley, and wheat required cultivation. After unloading the food stuff (flour, molasses, and sugar) to the cold cellar, he unharnessed the horses and let them into the pasture. Heading to the house with a brown box under his arm, he smiled to himself. In the kitchen, he set the box on the table.

Hannah looked at him quizzically, "Vhat's this?"

"Something for your journey to see your sister." His eyes twinkled; the corners of his mount twitched.

"Really?" Hannah eyed the fancy box.

"Come, open it," Fred encouraged.

She cautiously lifted the lid and peaked in. She burst out laughing, "I don't think this is for me." Nestled in a case made to fit was an Iver Johnson .32 caliber revolver.

"Yes, it is for you," Fred replied. "You can't be too careful on a stagecoach these days with highwaymen such a menace." He took it out of the box and held it in his palm.

"You can keep it in your purse." Overall, it was 5 inches long with a 2-inch barrel. He continued, "It's a special design by that Norwegian gunsmith, Iver Johnson, to be completely safe. The hammer lock prevents it from firing even if it is dropped. We'll set up a target to practice after dinner."

Levi and William returned from checking the fields in time for the noon meal. They examined the revolver with enthusiasm. "I heard it called a card table gun, accurate to up to 5 feet," William offered.

After dinner, the fellows set up a target—just a piece of paper with a red crayon drawing of a bull's eye. They attached it to a tree near the creek with a couple of nails. William went to the house, "Come on down, ladies, we're ready."

Hannah and Myrtle gathered the children and followed William down near the creek.

The adults and older children all took turns. Hannah smiled, "Vhat do you know, I hit the bull's eye the first time."

"You're a good shot," Fred Moses nodded. "I'll worry less, knowing you can protect yourself."

"Yes, it shoots straight and accurate," Levi agreed.

Note

1. Family stories don't say which sister Hannah was visiting or where it was. Gleaning other family history, it may have been Christine, who seemed to be closest to Hannah. Christine had become a Lutheran missionary in Iowa. She stayed in Iowa and married Samuel Sasai Lambert. They moved to Omaha, Nebraska. Christine died in 1923, leaving two sons, Samuel (15 months) and Joseph (two months). Fred Moses and Hannah went and brought the boys back to New Richmond and raised them.

34.

Moving Again

"If we're meant to stay in one place, we'd have roots instead of feet."
—Rachel Wolchin

By summer 1904, the crush of young'uns and adults was wearing. Five children under seven, including two toddlers, plus five adults stretched Hannah's tolerance. Some days her temper matched her red hair. She lashed out, "Esther, get these ankle biters out of the kitchen now before I whip the lot of you." Esther (7) grabbed Florence (4) and Ardis (2) by the hands and hurried outside. Art (6) quickly headed to the cow barn.

That night in bed, Hannah put her foot down, "Fred, this is too much. Ve must move."

Fred rolled over and hugged her, "I've been thinking that, too. I hear there's a farm to rent over on the road to Deer Park, about 3 miles from here."

"Oh, let's go have a look," Hannah squeezed his hand.

The house was small, containing a kitchen, the other room (parlor), and bedroom with room in the attic for sleeping. "Yust look," Hannah gestured, "a pump right at the sink. And there's room for the cots upstairs for the young'uns. The baby's crib will fit in the bedroom with us." With a sigh of relief, they moved.

William and Myrtle remained at Oakes Grove. When their second child was born, they named him Levi.

"Ah, you've given him a good name," Levi beamed. "We come from good stock, so little Levi will carry on those good traits."

"We thought you'd be pleased," Myrtle replied. "Pa, how many grandsons named Levi do you have?"

"Let's see…. Charlie and Anna have Levi Jefferson, plus Elmer Levi and Raymond Levi, and now we have another. It's good to carry on our fine name. I'm honored."

35.

The Last Will and Testament

"Our last will and testament, providing for the only future of which we can be certain, namely our own death."
—Hannah Arendt

The bell on the beveled glass door jingled as William opened it and held it for his father, Levi. The law office of Smith and Oakes was warm and inviting on this frigid day. The new building replaced the one that collapsed in the cyclone of 1899. Large windows facing the street were draped in deep maroon brocade. The floor was covered with a braided wool rug in shades of brown, black, and maroon. A small stove in the corner of the outer office radiated the heat of a blazing fire. Black leather settees were on both side of the stove.

Hearing the bell, George Oakes came from his inner office. "Mornin' Uncle Levi, William," he greeted them as he shook hands. "Here, let me take your Mackinaw, Uncle Levi."

"Thankee. I'll just stand by the stove a mite."

George hung the parka on the coat tree in the corner. "Uncle, it is good to see you. How have you been?"

"Oh, fair to middling."

George turned to William. "How was the road?"

"Fine for the cutter until we got to town. Too many goldarn ruts," William replied as he shed his parka and hung it up.

"Now, Uncle, are you warmed?" George inquired.

"Well, I'm startin' to thaw. This winter seems colder than usual for these ol' bones," Levi replied.

George observed how much Levi had aged since he had last seen him. His shirt hung loosely on his frail body; he was stooped, and his palsied gait was mostly a shuffle. "Come into my office and we'll go over your will. I have drawn it up as you wanted."

The three men sat around a round oak pedestal table. Across the room stood a massive oak desk, piled high with neatly stacked papers. Behind the table, the wall was lined with shelves of law books. George placed the will on the table in front of Levi and read it to him:

I, Levi J. Oakes, of the town of Richmond, in the County of St. Croix, State of Wisconsin, being of sound mind and memory, do make, publish, and declare this, my last will and testament, hereby revoking all former wills, bequests and devises by me made.

First: It is my will that all my just debts, funeral expenses, and all charges be paid out of my personal property.

Second: I give and bequeath to Brookins Heacock, the sum of five dollars ($5.00).

Third: I give and bequeath to my son William Oakes, all my personal property of every name and nature.

Fourth: I give and devise to my sons Silas P. Oakes, Charles A. Oakes, William Oakes, and Frederick M. Oakes, share and share alike, all my real estate of whatever description, that I shall died of, whatever situate.

In witness whereof: I have hereunto set my hand and seal on the 9th day of February, A.D. 1907

Levi J. Oakes

Signed, sealed, published, and declared by the said Levi J. Oakes as and for his last will and testament in the presence of us, who at his request, in his presence and the presence of each other have hereunto subscribed our names as attesting witnesses:

Fred A. Delamore, New Richmond, Wis.
John Jennings, New Richmond, Wis.
Geo. Oakes, New Richmond, Wis.

"Is everything as you wish?" George asked.

Levi nodded. "Fred and John should soon be here. I spoke to them a few days ago."

"No one knows where Brookins is?" George inquired.

"No, he had moved to Hudson. After his mother died, he never came home, and we lost contact," Levi responded.

The doorbell jingled. George rose and opened the door to the outer office. "Come in. Levi and I are ready for you."

Levi and William got up and shook hands with Fred Delamore and John Jennings. "John, you know your father was such a good neighbor to me for many years," Levi said.

"Father always spoke highly of you," John retorted.

Levi continued, "And just look at this nephew of mine—now he's a fancy lawyer graduated from the University at Minnesota. Can you beat this fine office, newly built after the cyclone?"

"Yah, we hear he's the best in town," Fred Delamore declared.

"Well, that depends on what side of the law you're on," George chimed in with a smile. They all chuckled. George went on, "Gentlemen, please be seated. Levi and I have gone over the will. It's all in order. So, I'll have Levi place his mark by his name and you fellows will sign as witnesses by your names."

He went to his desk and picked up an inkwell. It was a bronze structure fashioned like a throne. The center held a glass jar filled with indigo ink. The jar had a glass stopper. Two quill pens were held upright on the back corners. The inkwell was placed in the middle of the table. George removed the stopper, dipped a quill pen into the ink and handed the pen to Levi. He placed his index finger next to Levi's name. "Make an X right here."

Levi marked the document and handed the pen back to George. After blotting the ink, George passed the document, pen, and blotter to John and Fred. They signed it and returned it for George to sign. "Thank you, gentlemen. Now I'll put it in my safe and pray we don't need it for many a moon."

"Hump, these old limbs are a gettin' too much rhumitism. What do I owe you?" Levi questioned George.

"Why, Uncle, it's an honor—no charge."

"Boy, that's not right. You have a wife and son to support. I pay my debts. This is no different." Levi opened his wallet, carefully counted out five $1 greenbacks, and laid them on the table. "This new-fangled paper just doesn't seem like real money."

"It is easier to carry than gold pieces and works just fine," George laughed. He picked up the bills and handed two back to Levi. "You've overpaid."

Levi shook his head and returned the bills to the table. "Take some chocolates home to Carrie and Dale."

"Alright, Uncle, you win," George shook his head. The men bundled up, bracing against the brisk February day. "Keep this whipper snapper warm," George instructed William.

"I'll tuck him under the buffalo robe," William agreed.

George watched them go, musing, "Levi surely seems frail." Little did he know how soon the will would be activated.

36.

End of the Line

"Death does not mark the end of a chapter in a man's life, but the end of the book."

—Kilroy J. Oldster

"Was that a knock on the door?" Hannah looked at Fred. She sat in the wooden rocker near the cook stove, nursing Viola, just three weeks old.

"Can't tell with the March wind a howlin'," Fred responded. "Art, check the door."

Art sat up from where he was lying on the floor next to the stove and rose to go to the back door. "Bet it's just the wind," he called over his shoulder as he closed the kitchen door behind him. He crossed the washroom and cautiously cracked the back door. A blast of frigid air made him gasp. The person standing there was so bundled up, Art couldn't tell who it was. He pulled the door open. "Come in."

Once inside, the man unwound his green muffler to reveal his face.

"Why hello, Clyde. What brings you out in this weather?" Art, now nine years old, tried to sound grown up.

"I have a message for your pa." He struggled out of his Mackinaw and hung it on a hook. He bent over and popped the buckles on his galoshes and kicked them off. "I left Bessie in the barn to warm up."

"Fine," Art nodded. "Pa's in the kitchen."

Clyde had ridden from the store, about a mile down the road from Fred's farm. The store had the only telephone north of New Richmond; hence it was the neighborhood-gathering place for news and gossip, plus relaying messages.

"Well, hello, Clyde. Pretty poor weather to be out riding," Fred grinned. "Who's minding the store?"

"My ma's at the store. Pa said I best get over here. Your brother, William called. He said your pa died last night (March 8, 1907). They'll have the funeral on Sunday."

Fred caught his breath, turned away, and passed his hand over his forehead.

Hannah cried, "Oh." She covered her mouth with her hand as tears formed.

"I-I-I'm sorry to bring bad news," Clyde stammered.

Hannah recovered first. She quickly swaddled Viola and laid her in the cradle. "You must be frozen. Do sit and have a cup of coffee and a bite to eat." She bustled about, getting plates of bread, cheese, and butter.

Esther, now 10, got plates to set the table. "Come on, Flo, you can help. Get the cups."

"Me, too," Elsinore bounced across the room to carry the bread.

"Bobbie, do be careful, valk slowly," Hannah advised.

"Who's Bobbie?" Clyde inquired.

Hannah laughed, "That's Elsinore. Uncle Charlie dubbed her Bobbie 'cause she bobs everywhere—doesn't valk."

Everyone pulled chairs to the table. Hannah poured coffee for the adults. Esther poured milk for Art and little sisters Flo, Ardis, Bobbie, and Ruth. Flo lifted Ruth into the highchair.

"How was the road?" Fred asked.

"Oh, there was some drifting in open places. March is sure coming in like a lion," Clyde responded. He finished his coffee, bread, and cheese. "I'd best be going. Thanks kindly for the fixin's."

Fred jumped up and shook Clyde's hand. "Thank you for coming. I do appreciate it."

* * *

Sunday dawned clear and bitterly cold with a stiff north wind. At breakfast, Fred and Hannah discussed the day. "I can't take Viola out in this weather," Hannah exclaimed.

"No," Fred agreed. "I'll take Esther and Art with me. The little girls should stay here, too. Flo and Ardis are big enough to help."

Bobbie jumped off her chair; she hung onto the table and bobbed up and down, "I want to go, too."

"A big four year old like you can really help with your new sister," Hannah soothed.

"But I want to see them put Grandpa in the wastebasket," Bobbie wailed.

Everyone laughed until they cried.

"Art, let's get the cutter out. We'll take Mac. He needs a good trot." Mac was a driving horse that Fred was boarding for Harry Smith. The fellows bundled up and went to the barn.

"Esther, get six bricks from the cellar and put them in the oven," Hannah directed. They'll keep your feet warm on the ride."

By the time Fred and Art drove the cutter to the house, Esther was dressed and waiting. She was pleased with the cherry red wool cap and mittens that Ma had knitted for Christmas. She helped Art carry the hot bricks and place them in the straw that covered the floor of the cutter. They scattered straw over the top of the bricks.

"Get in and sit so your feet are on the bricks," Fred hollered against the wind. He took a couple of robes and tucked them around the children. "Pull your mufflers over your faces." He stepped up and pulled the buffalo robe over all of them.

With the clucking of the reins, Mac was off. He was a fast and willing runner, happy to be out of the barn. He shook his head and snorted. They made good time on the 5 miles from their farm to Oakes Grove where the wind wasn't as strong. They were glad to reach the warmth of the house, filled with uncles, aunts, cousins, friends, and neighbors.

Confused, Esther and Art stayed close to Fred and listened. People they didn't know shook Fred's hand and said things like, "I'm sorry for your loss" or "Levi was a great neighbor" or "I know you'll miss him." Some of the women were crying. Even their cousins were overcome with shyness and clung to their parents. The women folk brought food for the lunch after the service. The kitchen and pantry were filled with breads, cakes, cookies, and pies. The stovetop had many pots with great aromas filling the air.

Pastor Reynolds arrived. William met him. "Everything is ready in the parlor, but first have a cup of hot tea."

"Thank you. That sounds mighty good." After his tea, Pastor Reynolds called everyone to the parlor.

Esther took her pa's hand. Seeing the open casket, she hid her face against his side.

Art whispered, "It's just Grandpa. Everyone's looking at him."

Esther shook her head. "I can't look at a dead person."

Pastor Reynolds read from the Bible, prayed, and told what a good man Levi was. A lady sang "Rock of Ages." Then, they all said the Lord's Prayer.

Aunt Myrtle stood. "Please, come eat. Lunch is in the kitchen."

After lunch most of the people left. The four sons and their cousin George talked about moving the casket to the cemetery.

"The caretaker said he'd leave the building unlocked, so we could bring the casket in," William informed them. "The road seems open enough to get there."

The building at the cemetery had shelves to hold caskets of those who died during the winter when the ground was too frozen to dig graves.

"Maybe by April the ground will thaw," Charlie added.

"We can hope," Silas retorted.

Fred turned to Esther and Art. "Stay here while we take the casket to the cemetery, and I'll be back for you."

When the men returned, George called Silas, Charlie, William, and Fred together. "It was just in February that Uncle Levi asked me to draw up his will. It's here for you to read."

The brothers read the will, nodding approval.

"Has anyone ever heard from Brookins?" Silas asked.

"I heard he'd moved from Hudson—maybe up north," Fred offered.

They sat, each with their own thoughts. "Just look at us," Charlie mused. "Pa always said we come from good stock. He lived to the ripe old age of 82 and was healthy as a horse. Look at us. We're all healthy, upstanding citizens, blessed with wonderful families. We can be proud of what our ancestors passed on to us."

The Republic Voice, *March 9, 1907*

TWO PIONEERS PASS AWAY
LEVI OAKES NEARLY NINETY
AND MRS. M STEVENS AGED EIGHTY-EIGHT.

Levi Oakes

Levi Oakes died yesterday morning at six o'clock at the home of his son William. He was born in Aroostook County, Maine, Aug. 1, 1817, coming to St. Croix County in 1851, or 56 years ago, more than half a century. His first wife, Mrs. Mary Haycock died about 35 years ago and he was married the second time to Mrs. Morgan. His surviving children are: Silas and Charles of Superior, and William and Fred who live in this vicinity.

Tho Mr. Oakes retired from active life some years ago, he was a prominent figure among the pioneers of St. Croix County. He was a successful farmer, open hearted and hospitable and very liberal in his gifts of any good cause.

For many years, he owned and operated Oakes' quarry which has furnished considerable rock for building purposes in this city.

The funeral will be held at the old home tomorrow afternoon at 2:00 o'clock.

—Microfiche collection
City Library, New Richmond, WI.

Notes

1. In Oakes and Relatives, 1974, Fred A. Oakes wrote that Levi's birth date is in error. By all his records, Levi was probably born about 1825. Fred A. cites the 1830 census of Penobscot County, Maine, where the boy "age 5 but less than 10," most likely was Levi. He had the birthdate on the gravestone corrected in 1970.

2. Family records list cause of death as bowel blockage.

EPILOGUE

Levi and Mary Potter Oakes

The four sons who survived to old age—Silas, Charles, William, and Fred—all remained in Wisconsin. Silas and Charles went to Superior and worked together as contractors moving houses and farming, while William and Fred farmed near the home place. The boys were 14, 10, 6, and 2 when their mother died in 1872. After she died, her son, Brookins Heacox, moved away and the family lost track of him until Charles read his obituary in the Superior newspaper. He died on April 26, 1922. The brothers and their wives all attended the funeral in Bruce, WI and connected with Brookins' children and grandchildren. For many years they held annual family reunions for the extended Oakes and Heacox families taking turns at their various farms. The first one was held June 4, 1922, at the home of Fred Moses and Hannah Oakes. The year after Levi died, William and Myrtle bought a farm near Balsam Lake and moved. Fred and Hannah again moved back to the home place.

The fabulous wheat harvest in western Canada in 1909 was the talk of the farmers at the Grange Hall. In the fall, Fred decided to go see for himself. He was so impressed with the thick stubble in the fields that he bought a half section of wheat land 5 miles northwest of Barons,

Alberta, Canada. He talked about the wonderful harvest they would have next year.

In the spring of 1910, the brothers sold Levi's farm. Fred sold all but two boxcars full of machinery, horses, cattle, and furniture. These boxcars were shipped to Barons and the family moved there with great expectations. It proved to be a disastrous year for farmers with the worst drought. No seeds sprouted. Hannah wanted to try to save her strawberries, so each night son Art pumped buckets of water for them, but they still withered and died.

By August, Fred and Hannah decided they couldn't stay. They sold the cattle to a neighbor and gave things away, returning to New Richmond with only one boxcar full of possessions.

They rented a house near New Richmond for the winter. In the spring, Fred went searching for a place. He bought 40 acres north of Bunyan in Georgetown Township. All the pine had been cut, but the stumps needed to be removed. Fred and his son, Fred Arthur (always called Art), age 13, began the backbreaking task. Some of the stumps were 3-4 feet in diameter, so they dug holes under the stumps and set off dynamite. Each time a piece of adjoining land was for sale, Fred bought it, thus enlarging the farm to 160 acres. The family would live there until 1943 when they sold the farm and built a small house near Luck, Wisconsin.

Fred and Hannah had six girls and two boys. Five remained close to home. Four of the girls—Esther, Ardis, Elsinore, and Ruth—became teachers; Florence went to nurses training in St. Paul, Minnesota, then married a farmer and lived near her parents; and Viola went to Minneapolis and worked for Honeywell Company.

Fred Arthur went to Minneapolis and became an auto mechanic. Esther took Elsinore to Phoenix, Arizona, in about 1922. The doctors said the dry climate would help Elsinore's asthma. Both sisters married there and moved to Hayward, California, where their husbands' jobs took them. Esther continued her education in special education and writing learning handbooks for her "exceptional children." She told me that she went into special education because of her youngest sister, Viola, who was considered "slow"; however, she could manage money well, so Esther thought Viola just needed a different kind of education. Elsinore stopped teaching when she married. To support the war effort, she applied to Friden Company. She tested high in mechanical and design aptitude. She designed business machines. She worked for Friden until her death in 1948, receiving high praise for her designs. The company president called her one of their best engineers.

Fred and Hannah's youngest son, Hollis (always called H.E.) was to inherit the farm. He married Helen Wurtz, April 30, 1938. They moved in with Fred and Hannah. H.E. hated farming and it was a trial for Helen to be watched all the time by her mother-in-law and two sisters-in- law. They moved to Minneapolis where H.E. completed an apprenticeship as a steamfitter. He was drafted for World War II in 1943. Just before he was to ship out to the South Pacific, he received a telegram informing him that he was being deferred to go to Hanford, Washington to supervise the pipefitting contract on a new U.S. Army facility, the Manhattan Project. DuPont was awarded the general contract because of their strong safety record in building chemical plants. H.E. had supervised the pipefitting on some of those and had received many safety awards. Hence, DuPont requested him. It was top secret with a daily codebook for the next day's work. Because of all the Pyrex glass piping, H.E. knew they were building a toxic chemical plant. At the time only a few top engineers knew they would be enriching uranium to ship to Las Alamos to build the first atomic bomb. Today it is the Hanford Atomic Energy Center.

After the war, H.E. and Helen with their children, Bruce and Kay, returned to Luck, Wisconsin. While their house was being built, they lived with Fred M. and Hannah. Hannah spoke Norwegian with her sisters-in-law and neighbors. She spoke to me in Norwegian, too. If I did something Hannah didn't like, she would say, "Er du en lille Svenske pige?" Twenty years later, after living in Denmark, I could understand some Norwegian. Standing on a street corner in Oslo, I heard a woman say that to a girl about 10: "Er du en lille Svenske pige"—Are you a little Swedish girl? I laughed so hard!

H.E. and Helen loved the West. In 1948, they moved with their children (Bruce, Kay, and Launa) to Oregon and the next year to Moscow, Idaho.

H.E. always talked about the importance of having a son to carry on the family name since Bruce is the only Oakes grandson of Fred and Hannah. H.E. would be proud that his son, grandson, and great-grandson also became steamfitters. He died in 1997.

Sixty-three years to the day after Fred and Hannah were married, grandson, Bruce, married Alice Smith on February 13, 1959. They named their son Levi Shane, the seventh Levi after Nathaniel Oak arrived in Massachusetts in 1660. Levi Shane died September 19, 2016, of sudden cardiac arrest. His one son, Kenneth, survives him to carry on the Oakes name, but he has only daughters, the 11th generation since Nathaniel Oak. The descendants of Levi Jefferson who carry the Oakes name are those of his other sons: Silas, Charles, and William.

This tradition of only following the sons was rejected by Henry Lebbeus Oak in 1906. He wrote that he could see no reason to accept the tradition of genealogists to follow only sons. "Why should we reject the female lines if we care for family at all?" Such forward thinking! However, with the many branches of the family, I only followed my direct Oakes line from Levi Jefferson. Fred Arthur's book, Oakes and Relatives, 1974, follows as many lines as he could. In 1906, Henry Lebbeus Oak wrote that "the Oak, Oaks, Oakes tribe numbered about 20,000." Seeing such large families of the earlier Oakes's, today there will be thousands more.

One interesting distant cousin is Sir Harry Oakes (1874-1943). He is in the same generation as Fred Moses (1870-1958). They both had the same great-great-grandparents, Captain Jonathan Oak and Abigail Whitney Rand. Sir Harry had a most adventurous life as a gold prospector/miner in Canada, claiming the largest mine in Canadian history, the Lakeshore Gold Mine, in Kirkland Lake, Ontario. At one time he was the richest man in the world. In a fight over Canadian taxes, he moved to Great Britain. His philanthropy there got him made a Baronet, July 27, 1939, by King George VI. Harry moved to the Bahamas where he was brutally murdered. It is still an unsolved murder. Esther Oakes Carson (daughter of Fred Moses and Hannah) collected newspaper and magazine articles plus letters from Dover-Foxcroft, Maine, where Sir Harry's parents and siblings lived. Several books have been written about him. Descriptions of his jovial but also sometimes brusque and explosive personality reminded me of my father, H.E.

Names were a challenge because babies were often named to carry on a name or in memory of one who died. There are so many Marys, Levis, Williams, and Jonathans.

Timothy and Angelina Pishon Oakes Family

The spirit of adventure that had brought Timothy and Angelina to Wisconsin from Maine was passed on to their children. Timothy died in 1885, at age 64. Angelina followed three of their children—Prince, John, and Ray—to Chelan, Washington. She lived there until she died in 1914, at age 84. All but two of the children scattered westward. Frank and Della went to California; Lewis went to Arizona; and Leon went to Minnesota. Their younger daughter, Ida, died in 1878 at age 15. Their son, George, remained in New Richmond, Wisconsin for most of his life. He was their bookworm. He went to the University of Minnesota Law School and returned to New Richmond to practice law. He served two terms in the Wisconsin legislature in the 1920s. He married and had one son, Dale, a bachelor.

Four of their seven sons—Frank, John, Lewis, and Ray—remained bachelors. The three that married were Prince, George, and Leon. Prince had four children and his descendants still live in western Washington. Leon had nine children; one died at birth, five remained in Minnesota and Wisconsin, and three moved to California. Their daughter, Della, lived in Pasadena, California.

ACKNOWLEDGMENTS

Most of the chapters are based on family stories. Chapters 12, "Northern Lights" and 29, "Cyclone 1899" were my creation. Although I heard no family stories regarding these events, they are widely known to have affected everyone. Clearly my aunts and uncles would have remembered stories of those events had I known to ask before they died. I am indebted to my uncle, Fred Arthur, for conversations and his book. The story Uncle Fred told me about an Indian woman nursing Levi differs from other accounts in family papers. I am awed by the depth of his research. My Aunt Esther, who started the research, kept all her documents and notes. In the 1940s, she hired a genealogist in Boston, Dr. Mary Lowell. I have her hand-written notebook pages tied together with a blue satin ribbon.

There are many people who have contributed to this book.

Carol Purroy, who taught an adult education class, Life Stories, guided me to reach beyond my technical writing background.

Mary and Irving Sather, of the New Richmond Heritage Center, took me to see the property owned by Levi Jefferson. Irving knew that there was a family connection by marriage from his ancestor to my Great Uncle Charles. The New Richmond Heritage Center is located on property originally owned by Timothy Oakes, just across Paper Jack Creek from that of Levi.

James Reppe, also of the New Richmond Heritage Center, walked with me around Levi's farm, which is now a city park. Where the farmhouse stood is a playground. Farthest away along Paper Jack Creek are the walls of the horse barn, now being restored by the New Richmond Heritage Center. Just beyond the barn, the gently sloping hill is where the old lime quarry has eroded away. James recalled that when he was a teenager, the kids skied off the cliff that used to be there. James showed me how to access his Oakes file in the microfiche collection at the Public Library.

Pam Nelson Peterson, my cousin and the granddaughter of Fred Arthur Oakes, provided information and direction to the genealogy website Family Search, where she has entered much of the data on the Oakes family. She has all her grandfather's extensive notes and copies of his book, Oakes and Relatives.

All the members of the Thompson Peak Writers Workshop of Susanville, California, were so helpful in critiquing chapters of the manuscript, especially Margaret Liddiard and Kristin Volberg, who read the entire manuscript.

My mother, Helen Wurtz Oakes, now deceased, and I revisited many of the Wisconsin farms on a trip in 2010. She kept up the family history until her death in 2020.

My daughter, Sheryl Oring, encouraged my endeavor by sending books on writing historical books.

Granddaughter, Shira Emanuel, at age nine, made a bookmark "Write On."

My husband, Lewis Oring, gave constant encouragement, reading, and critiquing many drafts.

Dr. Ross Tangedal, Director and Publisher of Cornerstone Press, Ellie Atkinson, Editorial Director, plus all the student editors have been very encouraging and helpful. Their diligent editing and suggestions made the story better.

For all of you, I am grateful.

*Detailed family trees are available from the author. Please email: keoring@hotmail.com

SOURCES

Andrews, Christopher Columbus. *Letter of Tour through the North-West. In the Autumn of 1856. From St. Paul to Crow Wing, MN.* http://genealogytrails.com/main/stagecoachtrip2.html accessed 05/21/2021.

Bergland, Martha. *The Birdman of Koshkonong: The Life of Naturalist Thure Kumlien.* Madison: Wisconsin Historical Society Press, 2021, p. 70.

Bettmann, Otto L. *The Good Old Days—They Were Terrible.* New York: Random House, 1974.

Boehm, A.G., Mrs. "History of the New Richmond Cyclone of June 12, 1899." (St. Paul, Minn: Dispatch, 1900); online facsimile at http://www.wisconsinhistory.org/turningpoints/search.asp?id=1543

Carrington Effect. https://www.history.com/news/a-perfect-solar-superstorm-the-1859- carrington-event Accessed 04/10/2009.

Chas. Young & Oliver Gibbs. Pamphlet, 1856. http://www.wisconsinhistory.org/wlhba/articleView.asp?pg=1&id=12502&hdl=&np=&adv=yes&ln=&fn=&q=&y1= &y2=&ci=&co=Pierce&mhd=&shd= Accessed 5/25/21

Cyclone in New Richmond, 1899. https://archive.json-line.com/news/wisconsin/122784778.html/Accessed Sept. 8, 2021.

Diphtheria in Wisconsin, 1890s: http://www. burnettcountysentinel.com/news/diphtheria-in-burnett-county-burnett-county-history/ article_99487f02-c041-11e9-9bfc- 9f3313cfc8d4.html Accessed 5/15/2022

Epley, Anna P. *A Modern Herculaneum: Story of the New Richmond Tornado.* Published by author, 1900. Digitized 05/01/2008 by Google Books.

Fanning, Susan. *American Local History Network – Wisconsin Local History Network-Eau Clair County.* https:// www.usgennet.org Accessed 06/12/2021

Foote, Sarah. *A Journal Kept... while Journeying... from Wellington, Ohio to... Wisconsin, April 15 to May 10, 1846...*(Kilbourne, Wis: s.n., 1905); online facsimile at http://www.wisconsinhistory.org/turningpoints/search. asp?id=32 Accessed 05/21/2021.

Gray, Charlotte. *Murdered Midas: A Millionaire, His Gold Mine, and a Strange Death on an Island Paradise.* Toronto: Harper Collins Publishing, 2019.

Hadley, Craig, ed. *A Nineteenth Century Slang Dictionary.* http://mess1.homestead.com/Nineteenth_ Century_Slang_Dictionary.pdf

Holmquist, Jeff, ed. *New Richmond Wisconsin: The First 150 Years: 1857 -2007.* New Richmond, WI: New Richmond News Publication, 2007.

Houts, Marshall. *King's X: Common Law and the Death of Sir Harry Oakes*. New York: William Morrow & Co. 1972.

Hynd,Alan. *Who Killed Sir Harry Oakes? Book Length Feature, True, The Man's Magazine*, February 1952. Greenwich, CT: Fawcett Publications.

"Indian Murderers in Minnesota," *Harper's Weekly*, Dec. 20. 1862. http://www.sonofthesouth.net/leefoundation/ civil-war/1862/december/minnesota-sioux- massacre. htm Accessed 4/08/2011

Intensive Survey Report, New Richmond, June 1983. *Approximate Path of the June12, 1899, Tornado*, Monthly Weather Review for July 1899.

Kettner, Carol J. *The Pierce County Fair, 1883–1983*. Univ. of WI-River Falls.

Language of the Woods. *Logging camp diversion and humor. The lumber camps of long ago. Chippewa Falls*. http://homepage.mac.com/wieganbr/logging.html Accessed 3/18/09.

Independent, Jan. 14, 1915, www.scils.rutgers.edu

McCutcheon, Marc. *The Writer's Guide to Everyday Life in the 1800's*. Cincinnati, OH: Writer's Digest Books, 1993.

Morton, W. E. et. al. (Wisconsin State Centennial Committee, 1948). Online facsimile at http://www. wisconsinhistory.org/turningpoints/search.asp?id=1675 Accessed 6/10/21

New Richmond Heritage Center. *Not to be Forgotten: 1899 Cyclone: A Testimony of Survivors*. New Richmond, WI: New Richmond Heritage Center, 1999.

Oakes, Fred Arthur. *Oakes and Relatives*. Minneapolis, MN. Printed 1974.

Oakes, Levi Jefferson. https://www.familysearch.org/tree/pedigree/landscape/G8X8-2XH Accessed March 22, 2021

Oak, Henry Lebbeus. *Oak, Oaks. Oakes: Family Register Nathaniel Oak of Marlborough, Mass. and Three Generations of His Descendants in Both male and Female Lines*. Los Angeles, CA: Out West Co. 1906. Digitized by Google books, Oak_Oaks_Oakes.pdf

Olson, Eleonora and Ethel. *Yust for Fun: Norwegian-American Dialect Monologues*. Minneapolis, MN: The Lund Press, 1929

Reppe, James D. and Sather, Mary A. *Neighborhood Series: Down on the South Side*. New Richmond, WI: New Richmond Heritage Center, 2008.

Sather, Mary A. *They Built Their City Twice: A History of New Richmond, Wisconsin*. New Richmond, WI: New Richmond Preservation Society, Inc., 1998

The Republican, June 29, 1899, New Richmond, WI. Viewed on microfiche at the New Richmond Library, 05/02/2014.

Slang used by the lumberjacks. http://homepage.mac.com/wieganbr/slang.html Accessed 03/18/09.

Wisconsin Outline map, courtesy of the State Cartographers Office, University of Wisconsin, Madison. https://www.sco.wisc.edu/wp-content/uploads/2018/03/cnty_nm.pdf Accessed 5/1/21. Wisconsin Historical Society, Creator: Chicago and Northwestern Railway Co. Map of Stagecoach routes and locations of taverns, Image ID: 88478. Viewed online at: https://www.wisconsinhistory.org/Records/Image/IM88478 Accessed 5/20/21

Verified birth of Brookins Heacock in 1860 census as Brookins Oaks in the household of Levi Jefferson Oaks. https://www.familysearch.org/ark:/61903/3:1:33S7-9BSX- 999Q?i=4&cc=1473181&personaUrl=%-2Fark%3A%2F61903%2F1%3A1%3AMW9X-P92 accessed 03/07/2022

APPENDIX

"The Golden Wedding"

The years have passed and they have reached a milestone,
Fifty years and now our friends are growing old,
And so we've gathered here on this occasion
To celebrate the "Wedding Day of Gold!"

To share something better far than gold or silver
Fellowship that's warm and true and ne'er grows cold
Happiness of friends and family gathered round them
Is dearer than the clink of yellow gold.

To every life there is a story so they tell me
And there are questions you would doubtless like to ask,
So let us go back many years to the beginning
And I'll tell you how this marriage came to pass.

She was working in the village of New Richmond,
And the word had gotten round of Hannah's skill—
So Fred's Step-Ma sent him there to interview her
And it seems he plead their case with right good will.

A right likely looking boy so she consented—
Feeling as she rode beside him no alarm,
And young Hannah from the start seemed quite contented
As the helper at Oakes Lodge, the family farm.

And that is how in those hard early years
He found her so efficient strong and neat,
He came to know her thru laughter and tears,
And found her biscuits just couldn't be beat!

At "Oakes Lodge" in dead of winter they were married,
February 13th-eighteen hundred ninety-six
And as the knot was tied young Fred was heard to whisper "
Now no slipknots, please, or other fancy tricks!"

Hannah stood there straight and proud (tho' slightly nervous)
In her lovely gown of dark and lustrous green,
Her hair a shining mass of burnished copper,
And to Fred she was more lovely than a queen.

Rev. Snodgrass was the minister, so they tell
Who gave to Fred young Hannah as his wife
And he must have done the job up very well
To hold thru fifty years of married life.

The first four years were on a forty-acre farm
Here Esther, the oldest, and Fred Arthur were born,
Then along came baby Florence, without undo alarm-
For a childless marriage then was held in greatest scorn.

Next came baby Ardis, shy little elf-
Then blood poisoning nearly took poor Hannah's life
"What will I ever do without her?" Fred asked of himself –
As he gazed on his suffering wife.

But God spared her to them for he knew her great worth –
To her husband and wee helpless babes,
There was much to be done on the great, busy earth
So this good mother's life it was saved.

Elsinore came next, a beautiful child –
Her sunny nature chased away the gloom,
She had the form of "Aphrodite" and a manner sweet and mild.
They called her "Bobbie" 'cause she bobbed from room to room.

Next came Ruth and then Viola, two cunning little girls –
The family grew and prospered, all was well,
Then came that tragic day when the "demon fire" held sway
And their cozy home in blackened ruins fell.

Clothes and furniture were lost, and at what a fearful cost,
As they shivered in the cold of late November,
But kindly neighbors took them in, gathered up some things and then
Helped build a shelter near the lately blackened embers.

But this story grows too sad- there was good as well as bad –
There were incidents that touched their sense of humour
Like the day so hot and still, with his berry pail to fill
Fred ventured forth because he'd heard a rumour.

He'd just found a lovely spot, and to him it mattered not
That the sun upon his back was fiercely burning –
All around him on the bushes, hung the berries back and luscious
Then, right his way, he saw some women turning.

Quick he sprang behind a bush – and the thought came with a rush
"To get these berries I must be a clever fellow"
Then he played a little trick and laughed 'til he was nearly sick
 To see them run as loud and fierce that bull did bellow.

Hannah too loved picking berries – so with sister Bertie and the baby
Hitched up old King and with the buggy started forth –
When homeward bound King did falter–stood like the rock of Old Gibraltar
Tho' they urged him and commanded until hoarse.

Now Hannah knew the horse was clever, and that she must now endeavor
To get and see what made him act so strange,
A broken tug she saw before her – but she didn't let it floor her
Just quickly reached to see if baby had a "change".

Now picking berries is a very common hobby –
Shared by many, not by these good folks alone
But there's a few of us can say, looking back along the way
That a diaper drew our buggy safely home.

In 1910 to Canada they journeyed,
But misfortunes and disappointments there were rife –
So back to old Wisconsin in the autumn
To buy a home and have a settled life.

In 1912 the stork paid them a final visit,
And that little bundle brought them greatest joy,
For of girls they had an even half a dozen –
So they welcome this long looked for second boy.

The named him Hollis and he gave them much enjoyment,
And a minimum of trouble so they say –
At their home in Georgetown now the years were passing
And the children growing up to go away.

Of the six girls four had chosen to be teachers
A fifth to be a nurse in starchy white,
Now the sixth had no desire for making speeches –
She loved to cook and say! Her bread was fairy light.

All went well and then a sudden sorrow
Threw it's shadow on the home one fall day –
Two little boys were left without a Mother
When Hannah's sister Christine passed away.

Eight children of their own and Fred and Hannah
Were growing weary now, no longer young
But they couldn't let those babies go to strangers
So they took them in and raised them as their own.

They grew and thrived and livened up the household
Which by now had smaller grown with passing years,
They played and scuffled – how their boyish laughter echoed
Thru the rooms that saw so much of joy and tears.

Their own children now were grown and mostly married
And gone to make their fortunes one by one
Then sweet Ardis always delicate and fragile
Passed away at home in August '31.

Once again the spacious rooms were filled with sadness,
With the passing of this one so dearly loved –
Yes, the home where she was wed in all her gladness
Saw her soul's release to that new home above.

Fred and Hannah felt the weight of each new sorrow,
But time and work assuage our wounds as we all know
So they gathered up the reins and seemed to borrow
Hope and strength to start anew after each blow.

Dame Fortune had a stubborn way of ducking
Her obligations when poor Fred would need her most –
But her daughter Mis-fortune was in there plugging,
And followed him from pillar unto post.

To broken limbs she gave him painful introduction
When the frightened team of horses ran away –
And when as Carpenter intent on is construction
From the ladder or the scaffold fell away.

Periods of irksome rest while bones were mending-
Then another job he would be sure to try,
He would smile and think "my bad luck must be ending"
Then a piece of steel would catch him in the eye.

Now Joe and Sam are fully grown and they leave the old sweet home,
They go out into the world to try their wings –
So the burden grows too heavy – Fred and Hannah then are ready
To sell the farm and the rest retirement brings.

Now rest is very well when we are weary
From hard and grueling labor all the day –
But continual rest soon made them very dreary
"Something must be done" we heard them say.

At the age when many folks are tired of doing –
And content to doze and idle in the sun,
They started with a will to reck an old house
And from this to build a new and modern one.

Foot by foot and step by step it was accomplished –
Weeks and months of steady work 'ere they were thru,
 Now it stands, a monument to their great courage
Their little house! - and somehow their dreams come true.

There is always room for children and grandchildren –
When they come to spend a weekend with "the folks"
They planned it thus, because they knew it would be lonely
Without their laughter, visiting and jokes.

Fifty years! And may I add this in conclusion –
That gazing back across the span of joys and tears
It's been worthwhile, not just an optical illusion.
And we wish them many more bright happy years.

—Eleanor Espelien, February 13, 1946
(sister of Lillian Olsen Oakes, wife of Fred Arthur)

KAY OAKES ORING was born in Plum City, Wisconsin. Her family moved to Moscow, Idaho, but kept close contact with Wisconsin relatives, who sparked her interest in family stories. She taught college nutrition for many years before retiring to write full-time. She lives at Eagle Lake near Susanville, California, with her husband Lewis.